PINK SALT WEIGHT LOSS TRICK

WITH 100+ EASY RECIPES

The Natural Way to Lose Weight, Boost Energy, and Feel Lighter Every Day

Written by Mira Dane

© Copyright 2025 – All rights reserved Mira Dane

This publication is protected by copyright law and intended for personal, non-commercial use only. No part of this book—including recipes, design elements, or concepts—may be copied, reproduced, distributed, modified, or quoted in any form without prior written permission from the author or publisher.

The content presented in this recipe card is designed for informational and inspirational purposes, offering aesthetic and wellness-oriented culinary suggestions. While it includes approaches to hydration, digestion, and visual presentation, it is not intended to diagnose, treat, or prevent any medical conditions.

Users are encouraged to use the information mindfully and consult with a qualified health professional before making substantial changes to their dietary or wellness habits—especially if pregnant, breastfeeding, taking medications, or living with chronic health conditions.

The author and publisher disclaim any responsibility for adverse reactions, outcomes, or consequences resulting from the use or misuse of the content provided. Implementation of any ideas or recipes is done at the user's own discretion and risk.

This book is not a substitute for professional medical, nutritional, or mental health advice. When in doubt, please seek guidance from a certified practitioner.

TABLE OF CONTENTS

Introduction - The Pink Salt Method..7

PART I - THE FUNDAMENTALS THAT WORK

Chapter 1 - The Heart of the Method: Pink Salt..11

Chapter 2 - Weight Loss Isn't Just About Dieting..15

Chapter 3 - How to Find Your Direction...19

PART II - 100+ RECIPES TO ACTIVATE YOUR BODY

Chapter 4 - Morning Activation..25

    1. Morning Starter with Pink Salt and Lemon..26

    2. Warm Water with Pink Salt and ACV...27

    3. Pink Shot with Ginger, Lime, and a Pinch of Pink Salt....................................28

    4. Pink Latte with Coconut, Turmeric, and Pink Salt...29

    5. Saline Herbal Infusion (Fennel, Anise, Mint)...30

    6. Chia Seed Porridge with Cinnamon and Almonds...31

    7. Overnight Oats with Blueberries, Greek Yogurt, and Pink Salt..........................32

    8. Buckwheat Bread with Tahini and Banana..33

    9. Fluffy Frittata with Vegetables and Pink Salt..34

    10. Protein Pancakes with Egg and Chickpea Flour..35

    11. Active Water with Cucumber, Ginger, and Mint..36

    12. Energizing Infusion with Rosemary and Lemon..37

    13. Sparkling Water with Lime, Pink Salt, and Basil Leaves.................................38

    14. Detox Coffee with Pink Salt and MCT Oil..39

    15. Wake-Up Herbal Tea: Guarana, Cinnamon, and Orange Peel.........................40

Chapter 5 - Recipes to Debloat

    16. Green Soup with Fennel and Celery...42

    17. Zucchini Cream with Mint and Pink Salt..43

    18. Vegetable Broth with Kombu Seaweed and Turmeric....................................44

    19. Light Soup with Carrot, Onion, and Ginger..45

    20. Steamed Vegetable Purée with Flaxseed Oil..46

    21. Detox Water with Lemon, Sage, and Pink Salt..47

    22. Cold Infusion with Cucumber and Fennel Seeds...48

    23. Water with Grapefruit, Parsley, and Pink Salt..49

    24. Cleansing Water with Green Apple and Rosemary......................................50

    25. Warm Water with Bay Leaf and Lemon...51

    26. Orange-Turmeric Smoothie with Black Pepper...52

    27. Green Smoothie with Pineapple, Spinach & Ginger.....................................53

    28. Anti-Bloating Herbal Tea with Fennel & Anise...54

    29. Golden Milk with Pink Salt...55

    30. Antioxidant Smoothie with Berries & Chia Seeds..56

Chapter 6 - Regularity and Digestion..57

    31. Remineralizing Broth with Pink Salt and Seaweed.......................................58

    32. Chicken Broth with Vegetables and Apple Cider Vinegar..............................59

    33. Light Onion and Cumin Broth..60

34. Bone Broth with Pink Salt (Basic Recipe)..61
35. Warm Broth with Carrot, Celery, and Lemon...62
36. Warm Salad with Fermented Red Cabbage...63
37. Chickpea Hummus with Cumin and Pink Salt..64
38. Simplified Homemade Kimchi...65
39. Buddha Bowl with Sauerkraut and Toasted Seeds..66
40. Stir-Fried Tofu with Spinach and Tamari..67
41. Pink Salt & Flaxseed Gomasio..68
42. "Digestive" Dressing with Lemon, Olive Oil & Pink Salt..69
43. Toasted Seed Mix with Fennel & Cumin...70
44. Yogurt Sauce with Mint & Cucumber...71
45. Tahini Sauce with Garlic & Lemon..72

Chapter 7 - Burn Better Without Burning Out..73
46. Activated Almonds with Paprika and Pink Salt..74
47. Seed Crackers with Turmeric..75
48. "Spicy" Mix with Chili and Pumpkin Seeds..76
49. Baked Kale Chips...77
50. Avocado Lime Mousse...78
51. Chickpea Pancake with Avocado..79
52. Baked Lentil Balls...80
53. Spiced Pumpkin Cream with Pink Salt...81
54. Hard-Boiled Eggs with Hemp Seeds...82
55. Protein Wrap with Hummus and Raw Veggies...83
56. Liquid Vegetable Cream with Pink Salt..84
57. Warm Water with Pink Salt and Lime Juice..85
58. Lemon & Ginger Infusion...86
59. Mini Evening Vegetable Broth...87
60. Sip of Diluted Kefir with Pink Salt...88

Chapter 8 - Functional Proteins...89
61. Steamed Mackerel Fillets with Lemon and Pink Salt...90
62. Baked Salmon with Herbs and Orange Zest..91
63. Cod Soup with Ginger and Sweet Potatoes...92
64. Tuna Tartare with Avocado, Lime, and a Pinch of Pink Salt.....................................93
65. Warm Salad with Marinated Anchovies, Fennel, and Pumpkin Seeds....................94
66. Sweet Curry Chicken with Coconut Milk and Pink Salt..95
67. Turkey Strips with Rosemary and Lemon Zest..96
68. Bone Broth with Pink Salt, Carrots, and Ginger..97
69. Chicken Breast Salad with Green Apple and Red Cabbage.....................................98
70. Baked Lean Meatballs with Sweet Spices..99

Chapter 9 - Emotional Recipes...101
71. Dark Chocolate with Walnuts and Pink Salt..102
72. Coconut Pink Salt Popcorn...103
73. Apple Chips with Cinnamon..104
74. Frozen Banana Cocoa Mousse...105

- 75. Oat & Seed Mini Cookies 106
- 76. Energy Bites with Dates, Cocoa, and Pink Salt 107
- 77. Almond andSeed Bars 108
- 78. Apple Crumble with Almond Flour 109
- 79. Greek Yogurt with Honey, Cinnamon, and Pink Salt 110
- 80. Chia Seed Pudding with Berries 111
- 81. Sweet Potato Mash with Almond Milk 112
- 82. Light Risotto with Vegetable Broth and Lemon 113
- 83. Whole Wheat Pasta with Zucchini Cream 114
- 84. Miso Soup with Tofu 115
- 85. Polenta with Sautéed Tuscan Kale 116

Chapter 10 - Female Support 117
- 86. Pre-Ovulation Smoothie with Maca and Berries 118
- 87. Pumpkin Cream for PMS 119
- 88. Black Rice with Veggies for Post-Cycle Recovery 120
- 89. Almond Milk with Saffron for Mood Support 121
- 90. Pink Broth with Cabbage and Pink Salt 122
- 91. Spinach and Pumpkin Seed Frittata 123
- 92. Cyclical Red Lentil Soup 124
- 93. Sage and Lemon Tea for Day 1 125
- 94. Lemon and Ginger Risotto (Follicular Phase) 126
- 95. Oat and Banana Muffin (Luteal Phase) 127
- 96. Day 1 Drink: Pink Salt + Lemon + Honey 128
- 97. Calming Mix with Warm Water and Salted Chamomile 129
- 98. Morning Ritual with Saline Water and Maca 130
- 99. Pink Water with Hibiscus and Flaxseeds 131
- 100. Evening Tonic with Apple Cider Vinegar and a Pinch of Pink Salt 132

Chapter 11 - Bonus Recipes 133
- 101. Golden Kefir with Pink Salt and Fresh Ginger 134
- 102. Purple Beet & Tahini Hummus with Pink Salt 135
- 103. Baked Zucchini Chips with Smoked Paprika and Pink Salt 136
- 104. "Calm and Clarity" Herbal Infusion with Lavender, Lemon & Pink Salt ...137
- 105. Digestive Smoothie with Green Apple, Cucumber, Mint & Pink Salt ...138
- 106. Scrambled Eggs with Turmeric, Baby Spinach, and Pink Salt 139
- 107. Warm Plant-Based Milk with Vanilla, Pink Salt, and Raw Cacao 140
- 108. Warm Apple and Celery Soup with Pink Salt 141
- 109. Basmati Rice with Lemon and Mustard Seeds with Pink Salt 142
- 110. Avocado and Yogurt Sauce with Pink Salt and Lime Juice 143

PART III - YOUR NEW BALANCE
Chapter 12- Rediscover Yourself 147
Conclusion 153

INTRODUCTION
THE PINK SALT METHOD – NOURISH, ACTIVATE, TRANSFORM

This is not a diet book.

It doesn't promise miracles, nor does it ask you to count calories.

It's an invitation to reconnect with your body. To shift your perspective.

The heart of this book is a simple gesture: a glass of warm water with a pinch of pink salt.

But from there, a whole world opens up: the world of activation, awareness, hormonal and digestive balance.

Because often the problem isn't the food. It's the body in survival mode, the bloat caused by stress, the mental hunger, the disconnection.

And so Pink Salt becomes an activator—not just digestive, but also mental, emotional, and hormonal.

How the Book is Structured:

The book is divided into three major sections, guiding you from awareness to daily practice.

Part I – The Fundamentals That Work

Here you'll discover why Pink Salt isn't a trend but a powerful biochemical key, how it impacts hydration, pH, hormones, and digestion.

You'll also understand why losing weight isn't just about dieting, but about inflammation, emotional hunger, and chronic fatigue.

And finally, I'll help you recognize what your true goal is: maybe you don't just want to lose weight, but regain energy, mental clarity, regularity, and lightness.

Part II – 100+ Recipes to Activate Your Body

This is not a collection of "light" dishes.

These are recipes that nourish without overwhelming, designed to support your body through every phase: awakening, digestion, detox, PMS, cravings, mental energy.

Some include Pink Salt, others pair with it. All of them are practical tools to nourish yourself without punishment.

The recipes are organized by goal:
- Morning Activation
- Recipes to Debloat
- Regularity and Digestion
- Burn Better Without Burning Out
- Emotional Recipes (when you're craving something)
- Female Support (ovulatory, menstrual, luteal, post-cycle phases)
- Functional Proteins (meat and fish)
- Light Comfort Foods
- 10 Bonus Recipes to Mix Things Up and Experiment

Each recipe follows a simple and practical format: ingredients, instructions, and a real-world usage tip, so you'll know exactly when it can be most useful to you.

Part III – Your New Balance

Because knowing what to eat isn't enough—you also need to learn how to organize your life with kindness.

In this section, you'll find:
- How to create a functional weekly plan (routine, grocery shopping, basic prep)
- How to adapt meals based on your mood and energy levels
- The scientific foundations of the Pink Salt Method
- The weekly body-awareness journal
- Answers to the most frequently asked questions (real FAQs, no fluff)
- Glossary of key concepts (blood sugar, inflammation, hormones...)

This book is for you if...
- You're tired of punishing diets
- You want to feel truly light—without unnecessary restrictions
- You need energy, not less food
- You're looking for a guide that's practical but empathetic
- You want to build a new relationship with food—and with yourself

PART I
THE FUNDAMENTALS THAT WORK

CHAPTER 1
THE HEART OF THE METHOD: PINK SALT

Everything starts with a grain.
Or rather, with a glass of warm water and a pinch of Himalayan pink salt.

When I began, I wasn't looking for a "miracle cure." I was looking for energy.
I didn't want to lose weight at any cost—I wanted to get rid of that chronic fatigue that hit me as soon as I woke up, the brain fog that settled in after lunch, the sluggish digestion that left me bloated even after just a bowl of soup.
Then came that glass. And I started to study. And I discovered that behind that simple act, there was much more.

What Pink Salt Really Contains (and Why It Makes a Difference):

Himalayan pink salt is composed primarily of sodium chloride, like all salts. But what makes it special is the natural presence of over 80 trace elements and minerals: magnesium, potassium, calcium, zinc, iron, manganese...
These aren't miracle amounts, but it's a synergistic combination that can make a real difference when the body is depleted, inflamed, or simply "switched off."
Because the body needs conductors to function. Minerals do exactly that: they conduct signals, help cells communicate, regulate acid-base balance, fluid retention, cellular energy, muscle contraction, and digestion.
It's not the pink color that heals, but the harmonious combination of elements in a natural and bioavailable form.

Used wisely, Pink Salt is not a seasoning—it's an activator. A small amount, dissolved in warm water and taken at the right time, can support cellular hydration, stimulate digestion, and gently jumpstart your metabolism.

There are four main activation pathways, and they are:
hydration, pH balance, hormones, and digestion

1. Cellular Hydration

We often drink water but don't actually hydrate. Water on its own struggles to enter cells without at least a small presence of electrolytes (like sodium, potassium, and magnesium). Pink Salt helps retain water where it's needed.

When you're dehydrated at the cellular level, you may feel tired, bloated, foggy.

A small glass of salted water can get your system going again.

2. pH and Silent Inflammation

The body needs a balance between acidity and alkalinity. A chronic shift toward acidity (caused by stress, sugar, processed foods) leads to inflammation, emotional eating, and digestive blockages.

Pink Salt, along with fresh, plant-based foods, can help create a more alkaline, less inflamed environment.

3. Hormones and Metabolic Response

Salt isn't "the enemy of health"—it's a key regulator of hormones like cortisol and aldosterone.

When you're stressed, your body loses sodium.

When you restore mineral balance, your hormonal system can finally lower its defenses.

Ever noticed how you gain weight during stressful times, even if you're eating less?

Pink Salt doesn't eliminate stress, but it helps your body handle it better.

4. Digestion and Metabolic Activation

Sodium chloride is the base of hydrochloric acid in the stomach. Without a minimum dose of salt, your stomach doesn't function well.

That means fermentation, bloating, acid reflux, and poor nutrient absorption.

Taken at the right moment, Pink Salt can help rekindle your digestive "fire."

Answers for the Doubters: High Blood Pressure, Water Retention, and Common Myths

"But what if I have high blood pressure?"

This is one of the most common questions. And the answer is: it depends on the type of salt, the dosage, and the context.

Refined salt and the hidden salt in processed foods are the real problems. But a small dose of Pink Salt, taken away from meals and paired with plenty of water, can actually help regulate blood pressure—not raise it.

Clinical Insight:

Some studies suggest that moderate supplementation with natural salt, in people who are deficient, may actually improve blood pressure regulation by restoring the sodium-potassium balance.

For example, a study published in the Journal of Human Hypertension showed that using a potassium-enriched salt substitute led to a significant reduction in systolic blood pressure, as well as a decreased risk of stroke, major cardiovascular events, and all-cause mortality, compared to regular table salt.

Moreover, the Salt Substitute and Stroke Study (SSaSS) found that using a potassium-enriched salt reduced the risk of stroke by 14%, major cardiovascular events by 13%, and total mortality by 12%, compared to regular salt.

These findings suggest that moderate use of natural salts rich in potassium—like Pink Salt—can support healthy blood pressure regulation, especially when combined with proper hydration and a balanced diet.

However, it's essential to consult a healthcare professional before making significant dietary changes, particularly if you have pre-existing medical conditions.

"What about water retention?"

Water retention doesn't mean "too much water"—it means water is being held poorly. The body retains fluids when it's dehydrated or lacking in minerals. Pink Salt helps release stagnant water and re-establish a smoother internal flow.

"Isn't this just a trend?"

No. This is an ancestral strategy (just think of the salted broths our grandmothers used to make) that is now gaining scientific validation. It's not a miracle, and it's not marketing hype. It's a simple, natural, and powerful lever—when used correctly.

CHAPTER 2
WEIGHT LOSS ISN'T JUST ABOUT DIETING

Have you ever said: "I eat so little, yet I still gain weight"?

If so, you're not alone. It's one of the most common phrases among those who have been trying to lose weight for years. And the problem isn't willpower. The problem is perspective.

Because often, the body doesn't gain weight out of excess—it gains weight out of protection. Because it's inflamed. Because it's tired. Because it fears you're about to deprive it again. So it holds on. It shuts down. It resists.

In this chapter, we get to the heart of the matter: weight loss is a side effect of restoring balance. And that balance begins with three invisible enemies: **inflammation, emotional hunger, and chronic fatigue.**

We're not talking about pounds—but a weight you can feel, even when the scale doesn't budge.

1. Silent Inflammation

This is a state of chronic immune system activation. You don't have a fever, you don't have an infection, but your body is constantly reacting as if it's under attack. This leads to:

- persistent bloating,
- slowed metabolism,
- difficulty breaking down fats,
- water retention and out-of-control hunger.

Inflammation is fueled by sugar, ultra-processed foods, stress, and tissue acidification. Pink Salt, combined with a more natural diet, can help restore balance and create a less inflamed environment in the body.

2. Emotional Hunger

This isn't a lack of willpower. It's biochemistry.

When cortisol is high, your body craves sugar. When dopamine is low, you seek quick gratification.

But the more you respond with junk food, the more your body disconnects from true hunger.

Rituals like the morning drink with Pink Salt help to:
- provide calming minerals (like magnesium),
- reduce compulsive cravings,
- create a mindful gesture that breaks the automatic craving cycle.

3. Chronic Fatigue

A tired body doesn't lose weight—because everything in it is focused on **survival**.

And the first thing it cuts is **thermogenesis**—your ability to burn energy.

Do you wake up tired? Need coffee after lunch? Feel exhausted at night but still sleep poorly?

You might not need a stricter diet. You might need a nervous system that feels safe.

Cortisol, Leptin, Insulin: How They Get Blocked (and How to Unblock Them)

These sensations aren't in your head. And they're not just a matter of willpower or calories.

They are the result of a hormonal system that has lost balance—often due to stress, chaotic habits, and lack of internal listening.

In this section, we explore the three key hormones that influence **hunger, satiety, fat storage, and weight loss.**

Understanding them helps you stop fighting your body—and start working with it.

And the good news?

There are simple, natural tools to help reset the system—and Pink Salt is one of them.

CORTISOL: The Stress That Makes You Puffy

Cortisol isn't the enemy.

It's the hormone that keeps you alert, helps you react, and supports your survival.

But when it stays high—due to chronic stress or constant anxiety—your body reacts by:
- Storing fat (especially around the belly),
- Breaking down muscle to produce glucose (that "I'm losing weight but getting flabby" effect),

- Disrupting sleep and slowing down digestion.

The result?

You feel bloated even if you're barely eating.

How do you reset it?

Finding regular rhythms, eating to curb cravings, drinking a pinch of pink salt in warm water each morning, and carving out real breathing space (walking, journaling, silence) are the first steps to naturally lowering cortisol.

LEPTIN: The Hormone That Makes You Feel Full (But Only If It's Working)

Leptin is the signal that tells your brain: "I've eaten, I'm good."

But if you've been through years of yo-yo dieting, skipped meals, or lived under constant restriction, you may have leptin resistance.

What happens then?

- The brain no longer receives the fullness signal,
- You feel hungry all the time—even after eating,
- You feel like a "bottomless pit."

How do you reset it?

To help leptin get heard again, you need:

- A morning routine with Pink Salt → hydration + glycemic reset
- Fewer hidden sugars, more healthy fats and balanced meals
- No more forced fasting: it's better to listen to your body than punish it

INSULIN: When You Can't Lose Weight Because Fat Won't Unlock

Insulin is the hormone that "opens the door" to let glucose into your cells.

Need energy? Insulin delivers sugar where it's needed.

But if insulin is constantly elevated (due to frequent snacking, sugar, unbalanced meals), here's what happens:

- Your cells stop responding → insulin resistance
- Glucose stays in the bloodstream, doesn't enter the cells
- Your body stores fat and stops burning it

How do you reset it?

By reducing blood sugar spikes:
- Savory, balanced breakfasts—no more cookies and coffee
- Pink Salt water in the morning to stimulate digestion and regulate appetite
- Meals with protein, healthy fats, and fiber—not just "light" or "fit" options

When you begin to understand how your hormones communicate, you start working with them, not fighting against them.

Pink Salt, morning routines, small acts of awareness—they're not magic.

They're repeated choices that unlock chemical messages.

And through those messages, you also unlock your energy, your real hunger, your balance.

Pink Salt as a Metabolic "Switch"

It's not a magic wand—but it is a spark.

When used intentionally, it can help your body shift out of "survival mode" and back into "receptive mode."

It doesn't force your body to lose weight, but it allows it to.

How?
- By enhancing nutrient absorption (without taking in unnecessary toxins)
- By supporting deep internal hydration
- By boosting the production of stomach acid, enzymes, and bile
- By helping the nervous system find its point of balance

If metabolism is an engine, Pink Salt is the key that starts it.

And the rest—your habits, your food, your mindset—that's the fuel.

CHAPTER 3
HOW TO FIND YOUR DIRECTION

You don't have to lose weight. You need to feel better.
This book is not written to make you feel inadequate. It doesn't tell you that you need to weigh 20 pounds less or that you have to track everything you eat.
 It's here to help you reconnect with your body—and to help you feel better.

Because often what we call "weight to lose" is just another way of saying:
"I wish I felt lighter."
"I wish I had more energy."
"I wish my stomach wasn't always bloated."
"I wish I could stop fighting with my body."

That's why before jumping into the recipes, I invite you to pause. Not to look in the mirror—but to listen to yourself.

Your goal might be energy, lightness, regularity, clearer skin, or a better mood
Maybe you want to lose weight, but that might not actually be your body's real priority right now.

Maybe what you really need is:
- **Energy**, because you wake up already tired.
- **Regularity**, because your digestion is sluggish, inconsistent, or overactive.
- **Brighter skin**, because you feel dull, gray, "toxic."
- **More stable mood**, because you're riding a rollercoaster of hormones and blood sugar.
- **Lightness**, which isn't just about shedding pounds, but about releasing mental, emotional, and inflammatory weight.

Not all bodies want to lose weight right away. Some first need to heal.
And often, once healing begins, the excess weight naturally follows.

Mini Quiz: What Kind of Activation Do You Need?

Answer these short questions to get a sense of what kind of support may benefit you most. There are no right or wrong answers—just a compass to help you begin.

1. How do you feel in the morning?

A) Bloated and already tired
B) Hungry as soon as I wake up
C) No appetite, but mentally foggy
D) Physically okay, but instantly stressed

2. How is your digestion?

A) Slow—I feel full for hours
B) Sometimes too fast
C) Bloating even with small meals
D) Acid reflux or heartburn

3. What's your afternoon like?

A) Energy crash after lunch
B) Constant snacking, even without hunger
C) Emotional eating and mood dips
D) Brain fog, sugar or caffeine cravings

4. Which of these best describes your cycle (or general rhythm)?

A) Constipation or irregularity
B) Intense premenstrual cravings
C) Persistent abdominal bloating
D) Strong emotional swings throughout the month

Your Results (Just a Guide): What Type of Activation Do You Need?

Mostly A: Detox + Debloat

Your body needs to release, drain, and digest better. We'll focus on light recipes—soups, broths, detox waters, and simple salt-based mixes.

Mostly B: Regulation + Hunger Control

Your system needs to restore hormonal and blood sugar balance. You'll benefit from functional protein recipes, stable snacks, and "anti-craving" breakfasts.

Mostly C: Energy + Active Digestion

Your activation is sluggish. Energizing recipes will help—digestive salts, light spices, small metabolic boosters, and Pink Salt at the right time.

Mostly D: Calm + Mood Balance

Your nervous system is on high alert. We'll use calming recipes, foods naturally rich in magnesium, and rituals to regulate cortisol and sleep.

Your Body Knows Where to Go. You Just Have to Listen.

There's no need to force anything. When you give your body the right kind of activation, it responds. Always.

Now that you have a clearer sense of what your body truly needs, we can begin the most delicious part:

The recipes. Not "light," not depressing—functional, vibrant, and intuitive.

PART II
100+ RECIPES TO ACTIVATE YOUR BODY

When you pick up a book about Pink Salt, you might expect every recipe to include it. But that's not the point here.

The point is: what can you eat to help your body return to balance—without stressing it out, shutting it down, or loading it with anxiety or constant hunger.

Yes, many of these recipes include Pink Salt, and you can use it as a digestive activator, hydration regulator, or an ally in moments of disconnection.

But it's not mandatory. It's not the center of everything.

The center is you.

Your rhythm. Your energy level. Your true hunger.

That's why the recipes are divided by purpose.

Some help you de-bloat. Others stabilize your mood. Still others help manage emotional eating or rebuild after a stressful period.

The goal is not to "eat Pink Salt."

The goal is to find the gentlest, most effective way to stay present in your body as it transforms.

These recipes are here to support your journey—not complicate it.

They are tools, not rules. Support systems, not cages.

And above all: they're designed to nourish, not to punish.

CHAPTER 4
MORNING ACTIVATION

DRINKS WITH PINK SALT

1. Morning Starter with Pink Salt and Lemon

A small morning ritual that reactivates the body, rehydrates, and brings mental clarity. It's the first step back to yourself.

Ingredients
(Serves 1)

- 1 glass (about 7 fl oz) of warm water
- 1 teaspoon of fresh lemon juice
- 1 pinch (about ⅛ teaspoon) of Pink Salt

Instructions

1. Squeeze the fresh lemon and add it to the warm (not boiling) water.
2. Add the Pink Salt and stir well until fully dissolved.
3. Drink slowly, preferably right after waking up, on an empty stomach.

Recommended when:

- You wake up with a dry mouth or bloated belly
- You want to gently activate your digestion
- You're in the follicular phase of your cycle and feel drained
- You slept poorly or too little
- You want to start your day with a simple but powerful ritual

DRINKS WITH PINK SALT

2. Warm Water with Pink Salt and ACV (Apple Cider Vinegar)

Stimulates digestion, helps cleanse the liver, and reactivates metabolism. A simple routine to start your day in balance.

Ingredients
(Serves 1)

- 1 glass (about 7 fl oz) of warm water
- 1 teaspoon of raw, unfiltered apple cider vinegar
- 1 pinch (about ⅛ teaspoon) of Pink Salt

Instructions

1. Pour the apple cider vinegar and Pink Salt into the glass of warm water.
2. Stir well.
3. Sip slowly, preferably before breakfast or between meals.

Recommended when:

- You need to stimulate digestion
- You experience reflux or bloating after meals
- You feel heavy-headed in the morning
- You want to enhance mineral absorption and kickstart your metabolism

DRINKS WITH PINK SALT

3. Pink Shot with Ginger, Lime, and a Pinch of Pink Salt

A shot of natural energy: spicy, bold, activating. Your digestive "espresso" without the caffeine.

Ingredients
(Serves 1)

- 1 tablespoon of lime juice
- 1 teaspoon of freshly grated ginger juice
- 2 tablespoons of warm water
- 1 pinch of Pink Salt

Instructions

1. Grate the ginger and squeeze out the juice.
2. Combine all ingredients in a small shot glass.
3. Drink it in one quick sip, right after waking up.

Recommended when:

- You need a strong but natural metabolic wake-up
- You feel bloated or sluggish after a heavy dinner
- You're in the ovulatory phase and want to boost your energy
- You want a 30-second digestive mini routine

DRINKS WITH PINK SALT

4. Pink Latte with Coconut, Turmeric, and Pink Salt

Warm, creamy, anti-inflammatory. A morning (or evening) ritual that wraps you in comfort and helps you rebalance.

Ingredients
(Serves 1)

- ½ cup (about 5 fl oz) of unsweetened coconut milk (plant-based beverage)
- ½ teaspoon of turmeric powder
- 1 pinch of black pepper
- 1 generous pinch of Pink Salt
- Optional: ½ teaspoon of raw honey or MCT oil

Instructions

1. Warm the coconut milk in a small saucepan without boiling.
2. Add turmeric, pepper, and Pink Salt.
3. Stir well with a spoon or use a milk frother for a creamier texture.
4. Sip slowly, with presence.

Recommended when:

- You wake up with a tense belly or menstrual cramps
- You want a liquid, anti-inflammatory breakfast
- You're in the luteal phase and looking for a calming ritual
- You want to start the day with a caring, nourishing gesture—without solid food

DRINKS WITH PINK SALT

5. Saline Herbal Infusion (Fennel, Anise, Mint)

Delicate, aromatic, and functional: an infusion that deflates and helps the gut wake up gently.

Ingredients
(Serves 1)

- ¾ cup (about 7 fl oz) of boiling water
- 1 teaspoon of fennel seeds
- ½ teaspoon of anise seeds
- A few fresh mint leaves (or 1 bag of mixed herbal tea)
- 1 pinch of Pink Salt

Instructions

1. Make an herbal infusion by pouring boiling water over the herbs.
2. Let steep for 7–10 minutes, then strain.
3. Add the Pink Salt at the end, stir, and drink warm.

Recommended when:

- You wake up with bloating or abdominal cramps
- You skipped dinner or fasted the night before
- You want to gently reactivate intestinal transit
- You're looking for a simple way to reconnect with your body

ANTI-CRAVING BREAKFASTS

6. Chia Seed Porridge with Cinnamon and Almonds

A naturally sweet breakfast, rich in fiber and minerals, that keeps you full for hours without weighing you down.

Ingredients
(Serves 1)

- 2 tablespoons chia seeds
- ⅔ cup (5 fl oz) unsweetened plant-based milk (almond or oat)
- 1 teaspoon ground cinnamon
- 1 tablespoon slivered or chopped almonds
- Optional: 1 teaspoon Pink Salt (if the milk is very sweet)

Instructions

1. Mix the chia seeds with the plant-based milk in a bowl.
2. Add the cinnamon and let sit for at least 20 minutes (or overnight in the fridge).
3. When ready to serve, top with the almonds. You can enjoy it cold or warm.

Recommended when:

- You wake up hungry but want to avoid blood sugar spikes
- You have a busy morning and want to stay full for longer
- You're in the luteal phase and need balance between sweetness and satiety
- You're post-cycle and looking for slow, steady nourishment

ANTI-CRAVING BREAKFASTS

7. Overnight Oats with Blueberries, Greek Yogurt, and Pink Salt

A fresh, protein-rich breakfast ready when you wake up—perfect for packed mornings or when you're short on time.

Ingredients
(Serves 1)

- 3 tablespoons whole rolled oats
- 3 tablespoons full-fat Greek yogurt
- ¼ cup (2 fl oz) plant-based milk or water
- ½ teaspoon Pink Salt
- A handful of fresh or frozen blueberries

Instructions

1. In a jar or bowl, mix the oats, yogurt, liquid of choice, and Pink Salt.
2. Let rest in the fridge overnight.
3. Add the blueberries in the morning.
4. You can eat it as is or warm it up slightly.

Recommended when:

- You want a ready-to-go, satisfying breakfast
- You're hungry in the morning but want to avoid bread or cookies
- You want a high-protein meal without cooking
- You're in the follicular phase and looking for something fresh and stabilizing

ANTI-CRAVING BREAKFASTS

8. Buckwheat Bread with Tahini and Banana

Balanced, filling, and comforting—a naturally sweet breakfast that calms emotional hunger.

Ingredients
(Serves 1)

- 1 slice 100% buckwheat or whole grain naturally leavened bread
- 1 tablespoon pure tahini (unsweetened)
- ½ ripe banana, sliced
- A pinch of Pink Salt

Instructions

1. Lightly toast the slice of bread.
2. Spread the tahini, add banana slices, and sprinkle with Pink Salt.
3. Eat slowly, chewing thoroughly.

Recommended when:

- You feel the need to chew to calm nervous hunger
- You want something sweet but balanced
- You're in the premenstrual phase and craving comfort food
- You wake up feeling drained and need a grounding breakfast

ANTI-CRAVING BREAKFASTS

9. Fluffy Frittata with Vegetables and Pink Salt

A protein-packed, stabilizing breakfast that activates energy without triggering emotional hunger.

Ingredients
(Serves 1)

- 2 eggs
- Vegetables of your choice (e.g., zucchini, spinach, bell peppers)
- 1 teaspoon extra virgin olive oil
- 1 pinch Pink Salt
- Fresh herbs to taste

Instructions

1. Beat the eggs with Pink Salt and herbs.
2. Pour into a non-stick skillet with olive oil and finely chopped vegetables.
3. Cook over medium heat with a lid for a few minutes.
4. Serve warm or at room temperature.

When to Use This Recipe:

- If you want a protein-rich breakfast that truly satisfies
- If you're in the follicular phase and need clean energy
- If you need blood sugar balance first thing in the morning
- If you want to avoid the 11:00 a.m. cravings

ANTI-CRAVING BREAKFASTS

10. Protein Pancakes with Egg and Chickpea Flour

A savory alternative to sweet breakfasts, rich in protein and gluten-free.

Ingredients
(Serves 1)

- 1 egg
- 2 tablespoons chickpea flour
- 2 tablespoons water or plant-based milk
- 1 pinch Pink Salt
- Optional: rosemary or herbs of your choice

Instructions

1. Mix all ingredients until you get a smooth batter.
2. Cook in a well-heated non-stick skillet, forming 2 small pancakes.
3. Flip after 2–3 minutes and cook a bit more.
4. Serve with vegetables or a drizzle of raw olive oil.

When to Use This Recipe:

- If you want to start the day sugar-free but still flavorful
- If you're in the pre-ovulatory phase and need a protein boost
- If you wake up hungry but want to skip bread
- If you're looking for an alternative to classic sweet breakfasts

FUNCTIONAL WATERS AND ENERGY SHOTS

11. Active Water with Cucumber, Ginger, and Mint

Refreshing, cleansing, and light: a simple drink that reactivates without overstimulation and reduces bloating without draining you.

Ingredients
(Serves 1)

- ¾ cup (about 6.8 fl oz) room-temperature still water
- 2 thin slices of cucumber
- ½ inch piece of fresh ginger
- 3 fresh mint leaves
- 1 pinch of Pink Salt

Instructions

1. Place all the ingredients in a glass or jar and let it infuse for at least 10 minutes.
2. You can also prepare it the night before and drink it in the morning.

When to Use This Recipe:

- If you wake up with a foggy mind and a bloated belly
- If you had a heavy dinner the night before
- If you're looking for a hydrating but not boring drink
- If you need something cleansing and gently stimulating

FUNCTIONAL WATERS AND ENERGY SHOTS

12. Energizing Infusion with Rosemary and Lemon

Aromatic and tonic, it helps awaken the mind and bring clarity to disoriented days.

Ingredients
(Serves 1)

- ¾ cup (about 6.8 fl oz) boiling water
- 1 sprig of fresh rosemary (or ½ teaspoon dried)
- 2 thin lemon slices
- 1 pinch of Pink Salt

Instructions

1. Pour the boiling water over the rosemary and lemon slices.
2. Let steep for 5–8 minutes.
3. Add the Pink Salt at the end, stir, and drink warm.

When to Use This Recipe:

- If you feel sluggish and mentally uninspired
- If you're looking for a coffee alternative that helps with focus
- If you want to stimulate digestion with aromatic herbs
- If you're in the ovulatory phase and need direction and clarity

FUNCTIONAL WATERS AND ENERGY SHOTS

13. Sparkling Water with Lime, Pink Salt, and Basil Leaves

Refreshing and functional—perfect when you crave a fizzy drink that actually supports your body.

Ingredients
(Serves 1)

- ¾ cup (about 6.8 fl oz) natural sparkling water
- Juice of ½ lime
- 3–4 fresh basil leaves
- 1 pinch of Pink Salt

Instructions

1. Squeeze the lime directly into the glass.
2. Add the Pink Salt, pour in the sparkling water, and then add the basil leaves.
3. Drink immediately to enjoy the freshness and light effervescence.

When to Use It:

- On hot days when you need vibrant hydration
- If you're looking for a healthy alternative to soda
- If you crave something fresh but functional
- If you want to stimulate bile production and morning digestion

FUNCTIONAL WATERS AND ENERGY SHOTS

14. Detox Coffee with Pink Salt and MCT Oil

A coffee that nourishes and supports mental energy without the sugar crash or extreme fasting effects.

Ingredients
(Serves 1)

- 1 shot of espresso or strong brewed coffee (about 1.5–2 fl oz)
- 1 teaspoon MCT oil (or coconut oil)
- 1 pinch of Pink Salt

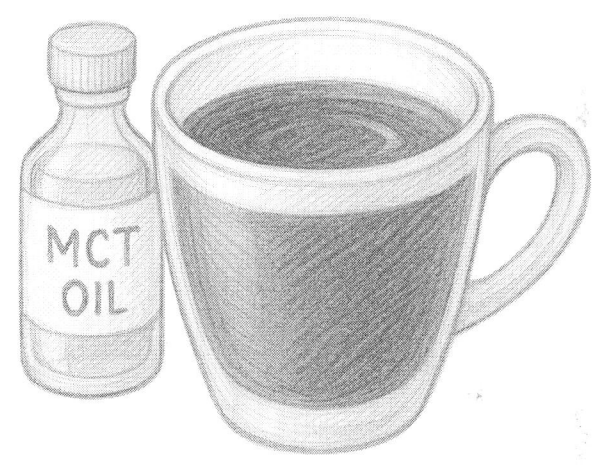

Instructions

1. Prepare the coffee and pour it into a cup.
2. Add the oil and Pink Salt.
3. Stir vigorously or blend with an immersion blender to create a smooth, creamy drink.

When to Use It:

- If you're doing a short fast and want to sustain mental energy
- If you want the benefits of coffee without the crashes
- If you're in ketosis or working out on an empty stomach
- If you're looking for "good fats" to curb morning hunger

FUNCTIONAL WATERS AND ENERGY SHOTS

15. Wake-Up Herbal Tea: Guarana, Cinnamon, and Orange Peel

Spices, stimulation, and warmth: an herbal tea that energizes the body and mind without creating nervousness.

Ingredients
(Serves 1)

- ¾ cup water (about 6.8 fl oz)
- ½ teaspoon guarana powder
- 1 cinnamon stick or ½ teaspoon ground cinnamon
- Organic orange peel (1–2 small strips)
- A pinch of Pink Salt

Instructions

1. Heat the water to about 160–175°F.
2. Add all the ingredients, stir well, and let steep for 5 minutes.
3. Strain if using a cinnamon stick or fresh orange peel.
4. Sip slowly.

My Recommendation

- If you want mental clarity without anxiety
- If you have a busy morning and want to start grounded
- If you're looking for a spiced, aromatic, and functional tea
- If you're in the pre-ovulatory or premenstrual phase and want stimulation without overstimulation

CHAPTER 5
RECIPES TO DEBLOAT

DRAINING AND REMINERALIZING SOUPS

16. Green Soup with Fennel and Celery

Debloating, light, and mineral-rich: a simple purée to release water retention without needing to fast.

Ingredients
(for 1 serving)

- ½ fennel bulb
- 1 stalk of celery
- 1 small zucchini
- 1 teaspoon extra virgin olive oil
- 1 cup (8.5 fl oz) water
- 1 pinch of Pink Salt

Instructions

1. Chop the vegetables and cook them in water for about 10–12 minutes.
2. Blend until smooth.
3. Add Pink Salt and olive oil only at the end.

Recommended when:

- You feel bloated after a heavy weekend
- You want a lighter dinner without giving up warmth
- You're in your premenstrual phase and feeling water retention
- You need a light dish that helps you "debloat without fasting"

DRAINING AND REMINERALIZING SOUPS

17. Zucchini Cream with Mint and Pink Salt

Smooth, refreshing, and detoxifying: a summer soup that drains without dehydrating and refreshes both body and mind.

Ingredients
(for 1 serving)

- 2 medium zucchinis
- 3–4 fresh mint leaves
- ¾ cup (6.8 fl oz) water
- 1 teaspoon extra virgin olive oil
- A generous pinch of Pink Salt

Instructions

1. Slice the zucchini and cook in a small amount of water for 8–10 minutes.
2. Blend with the mint until smooth.
3. Add Pink Salt and olive oil raw, just before serving.

Recommended when:

- You need internal freshness
- You want to drain without dehydrating
- You're in your ovulatory phase and need lightness and clarity
- You ate too much salty or spicy food the day before

DRAINING AND REMINERALIZING SOUPS

18. Vegetable Broth with Kombu Seaweed and Turmeric

Alkalizing, remineralizing, and rebalancing: a simple yet deeply effective broth.

Ingredients
(for 1 serving)

- 2 cups (17 fl oz) water
- 1 small piece of kombu seaweed
- ½ teaspoon ground turmeric
- 1 pinch black pepper
- 1 pinch of Pink Salt

Instructions

1. Bring water to a boil with the kombu seaweed.
2. Cook for 10 minutes.
3. Remove the seaweed, add turmeric, pepper, and Pink Salt.
4. Stir well and drink warm or hot.

Recommended when:

- You feel "toxic" or bloated all over
- You're having a digestive rest day
- You want a light, mineral-rich base
- You want to do a reset day without fasting

DRAINING AND REMINERALIZING SOUPS

19. Light Soup with Carrot, Onion, and Ginger

Warming and regulating, perfect for days when your body needs gentle heat without excess.

Ingredients
(for 1 serving)

- 1 carrot
- ½ small onion
- 1 small piece of fresh ginger (about ½ inch)
- 1 cup (8.5 fl oz) water
- 1 teaspoon extra virgin olive oil
- 1 pinch of Pink Salt

Instructions

1. Chop the vegetables and cook in water for about 15 minutes.
2. Blend or leave chunky, depending on your preference.
3. Season with Pink Salt and drizzle with olive oil raw.

Recommended when:

- You need to calm your belly and stomach
- You feel cold inside or heavy
- You want a simple soup that warms and rebalances
- You're in the days before your cycle and need comfort without bloating

DRAINING AND REMINERALIZING SOUPS

20. Steamed Vegetable Purée with Flaxseed Oil

A detoxifying and anti-inflammatory dish that nourishes without triggering emotional hunger: ideal for reset moments.

Ingredients
(for 1 serving)

- 1 handful of vegetables of your choice (e.g., zucchini, cauliflower, celery root)
- ¾ cup (6.8 fl oz) warm water
- 1 teaspoon cold-pressed flaxseed oil
- 1 pinch of Pink Salt

Instructions

1. Steam the vegetables until tender.
2. Blend with the warm water, then add Pink Salt and flaxseed oil at the end.
3. Serve immediately.

Recommended when:

- You want a detox and anti-inflammatory recipe
- You're in the luteal phase and want to lighten up without weakening yourself
- You want to drain without depriving your body
- You've had a full day and want to "wind down" with something warm and gentle

DETOX WATERS WITH DIGESTIVE ACTION

21. Detox Water with Lemon, Sage, and Pink Salt

A warm and functional water, ideal for draining, debloating, and reactivating the body without overstimulation.

Ingredients
(Serves 1)

- ¾ cup warm water (about 6.8 fl oz)
- 2 fresh sage leaves
- 1 teaspoon lemon juice
- A pinch of Pink Salt

Instructions

1. Steep the sage in warm water for 5 minutes.
2. Add the lemon juice and Pink Salt only at the end.
3. Stir well and drink warm.

Recommended when:

- You feel bloated after meals
- You need a gentle detox gesture
- You're in the second half of your menstrual cycle and feel water retention
- You ate a lot of dairy or starchy foods the day before

DETOX WATERS WITH DIGESTIVE ACTION

22. Cold Infusion with Cucumber and Fennel Seeds

Refreshing and digestive, great to sip throughout the day for a calming and debloating effect.

Ingredients
(Serves 1)

- 1 cup cold or room-temperature water (about 8.5 fl oz)
- 2 thin slices of cucumber
- 1 teaspoon lightly crushed fennel seeds
- A pinch of Pink Salt

Instructions

1. Combine all ingredients in a jar or small bottle.
2. Let it infuse for at least 1 hour (ideally overnight in the fridge).
3. Shake gently before drinking.

Recommended when:

- You feel bloated and heavy, especially after dinner
- You need hydration with a flat-belly effect
- You want a beverage to sip throughout the day
- You're in the premenstrual phase and retaining fluids

DETOX WATERS WITH DIGESTIVE ACTION

23. Water with Grapefruit, Parsley, and Pink Salt

Tonic and slightly bitter, it activates the liver and bile and helps you restart on days when you feel sluggish.

Ingredients
(Serves 1)

- ¾ cup plain water (about 6.8 fl oz)
- 1 teaspoon fresh grapefruit juice
- A few fresh parsley leaves
- A pinch of Pink Salt

Instructions

1. Mix the water, grapefruit juice, and Pink Salt.
2. Add the lightly crushed parsley leaves.
3. Let sit for 5–10 minutes and drink immediately.

Recommended when:

- You need to stimulate the liver and metabolism
- You want a detox that doesn't drain your energy
- You wake up with a coated tongue or bad breath
- You want a "bitter" drink that stimulates bile production

DETOX WATERS WITH DIGESTIVE ACTION

24. Cleansing Water with Green Apple and Rosemary

Aromatic, slightly fruity, and functional: supports digestion and helps reduce fluid retention.

Ingredients
(Serves 1)

- 1 cup plain water (about 8.5 fl oz)
- 2 thin slices of green apple
- 1 small sprig of fresh rosemary
- A pinch of Pink Salt

Instructions

1. Let the apple and rosemary infuse in room-temperature water for at least 15–20 minutes.
2. Add the Pink Salt at the end.
3. Drink cool or at room temperature.

Recommended when:

- You want a functional water to take on the go
- You want to counteract water retention and abdominal heaviness
- You feel bloated even after drinking plain water
- You want something aromatic, without sugar or acidity

DETOX WATERS WITH DIGESTIVE ACTION

25. Warm Water with Bay Leaf and Lemon

A deep detox gesture that soothes the stomach and liver and gently supports your morning reactivation.

Ingredients
(Serves 1)

- ¾ cup water (about 6.8 fl oz)
- 1 bay leaf
- 1 teaspoon lemon juice
- A pinch of Pink Salt

Instructions

1. Boil the bay leaf for 2 minutes, then turn off the heat and let it steep for another 5 minutes.
2. Add the lemon juice and Pink Salt only once the water is warm.
3. Drink slowly.

Recommended when:

- You're experiencing slow digestion or sluggish bowels
- You wake up with a tight stomach
- You want to start the day with a deep but gentle detox
- You're looking for a calming ritual for the liver and intestines

ANTI-INFLAMMATORY SMOOTHIES & HERBAL INFUSIONS

26. Orange-Turmeric Smoothie with Black Pepper

A powerhouse of natural anti-inflammatories with a fresh and spicy flavor—perfect for when your body feels under pressure

Ingredients
(Serves 1)

- 1 peeled orange
- ½ cup (3.4 fl oz) water or light plant-based milk
- ½ teaspoon turmeric powder
- A pinch of black pepper
- A pinch of Pink Salt

Instructions

1. Blend all ingredients until smooth.
2. Drink immediately to get the full benefits of the activated turmeric.

Recommended when:

- You need an anti-inflammatory and digestive boost
- You have muscle, menstrual, or joint pain
- You want something refreshing but not sugary
- You're in the luteal phase and feeling heavy

ANTI-INFLAMMATORY SMOOTHIES & HERBAL INFUSIONS

27. Green Smoothie with Pineapple, Spinach & Ginger

A detoxifying, vitamin-rich blend that supports liver cleansing, reduces bloating, and provides clean energy.

Ingredients
(Serves 1)

- 1 slice of fresh pineapple
- 1 handful of fresh spinach
- ½ inch piece of fresh ginger
- ½ cup (3.4 fl oz) water
- A pinch of Pink Salt

Instructions

1. Blend all ingredients until smooth.
2. You can strain it if you prefer, or drink it with the fiber for extra benefits.

Recommended when:

- You're feeling bloated or sluggish
- You want to detox without heaviness
- You've had a day full of sugar or refined carbs
- You're in the follicular phase and want clean energy

ANTI-INFLAMMATORY SMOOTHIES & HERBAL INFUSIONS

28. Anti-Bloating Herbal Tea with Fennel & Anise

A classic happy-gut infusion with a mineral twist: helps digestion and soothes abdominal discomfort.

Ingredients
(Serves 1)

- ¾ cup (6.8 fl oz) boiling water
- ½ teaspoon fennel seeds
- ½ teaspoon anise seeds
- A pinch of Pink Salt

Instructions

1. Steep the seeds in boiling water for 10 minutes.
2. Strain, add the Pink Salt, and drink warm—ideally between meals or after dinner.

Recommended when:

- You feel bloated after eating
- You struggle with constipation or intestinal gas
- You want a tea that truly works
- You're looking for an evening ritual without sugar

ANTI-INFLAMMATORY SMOOTHIES & HERBAL INFUSIONS

29. Golden Milk with Pink Salt

A warm, calming, and soothing drink—perfect for winding down your day while easing inflammation.

Ingredients
(Serves 1)

- ⅔ cup (5 fl oz) coconut or oat milk
- ½ teaspoon turmeric
- A pinch of black pepper
- A pinch of Pink Salt
- Optional: ½ teaspoon honey

Instructions

1. Warm the milk with turmeric and pepper.
2. Stir in the Pink Salt.
3. Do not bring to a boil.
4. Drink warm, slowly.

Recommended when:

- You feel internal inflammation, tension, or cramps
- You're in the premenstrual or menstrual phase
- You want something calming but nourishing
- You need a comforting evening ritual that doesn't trigger cravings

ANTI-INFLAMMATORY SMOOTHIES & HERBAL INFUSIONS

30. Antioxidant Smoothie with Berries & Chia Seeds

Bright and full of fiber and natural antioxidants—refreshing, satisfying, and perfect for lightness and regularity.

Ingredients
(Serves 1)

- 1 handful of fresh or frozen berries
- 1 teaspoon chia seeds
- ½ cup (3.4 fl oz) water or plant-based milk
- A pinch of Pink Salt

Instructions

1. Blend the berries with the liquid and Pink Salt.
2. Stir in chia seeds at the end and let sit for 5 minutes to let them swell slightly.

Recommended when:

- You're feeling dull or your skin looks tired
- You need a natural antioxidant boost
- You want to gently support digestion and regularity
- You're in the post-cycle phase and ready to feel light again

CHAPTER 6
REGULARITY AND DIGESTION

FUNCTIONAL BROTHS

31. Remineralizing Broth with Pink Salt and Seaweed

A simple and deeply nourishing broth, perfect for rehydrating the body and rebuilding from the inside during times of energy depletion.

Ingredients
(Serves 1)

- 2 cups water (500 ml)
- 1 piece kombu seaweed (about 1 inch)
- 1 generous pinch of Pink Salt
- optional: ½ teaspoon apple cider vinegar

Instructions

1. Bring the water and kombu to a boil and simmer for 10–15 minutes.
2. Turn off the heat, add the Pink Salt (and vinegar if using), and stir well.
3. Drink warm or use as a base for other preparations.

When to Use:

- If you're feeling drained or depleted after your period
- If you're on a detox day but need electrolytes
- If you want to gently and deeply support your gut
- If you're doing a partial fast and need to replenish

FUNCTIONAL BROTHS

32. Chicken Broth with Vegetables and Apple Cider Vinegar

Deep, rich, and comforting: a mineral-rich hug that supports digestion and nurtures during fragile times.

Ingredients
(Serves 1)

- 1 chicken thigh (bone-in)
- 1 carrot, 1 celery stalk, ½ onion
- ½ tablespoon apple cider vinegar
- 2 cups water (500 ml)
- 1 pinch of Pink Salt

Instructions

1. Place all ingredients in a pot and bring to a boil.
2. Simmer on low for at least 1 hour.
3. Strain or enjoy with the vegetables.
4. Add the Pink Salt at the end before serving.

When to Use:

- If you want a collagen-rich, complete broth
- If you're rebuilding or dealing with chronic fatigue
- If your digestion is slow or your gut is inflamed
- If you're looking for a comfort food that nourishes without burdening

FUNCTIONAL BROTHS

33. Light Onion and Cumin Broth

Light yet effective, this broth stimulates digestion and soothes bloating without overwhelming the stomach.

Ingredients
(Serves 1)

- 1 small onion
- ½ teaspoon cumin seeds
- 1¾ cups water (400 ml)
- 1 pinch of Pink Salt

Instructions

1. Quarter the onion and simmer it with the cumin seeds in water for 20–30 minutes.
2. Strain, add Pink Salt, and sip warm in small amounts.

When to Use:

- If digestion is blocked or you're feeling bloated
- If you want a light broth to sip between meals
- If you're in your ovulatory phase and want to feel lighter without fasting
- If you need to calm abdominal cramps or tension

FUNCTIONAL BROTHS

34. Bone Broth with Pink Salt (Basic Recipe)

Rich in collagen, minerals, and deep nourishment: the ultimate restorative broth.

Ingredients
(Serves 1)

- 2 beef or chicken bones with marrow
- 1 tablespoon apple cider vinegar
- 1 carrot, 1 celery stalk, 1 garlic clove
- 4 cups water (1 liter)
- 1 generous pinch of Pink Salt

Instructions

1. Place all ingredients in a pot. Bring to a boil, then simmer on low for at least 3 hours (6–8 hours is better).
2. Strain, add Pink Salt, and store in the fridge for 2–3 days.

When to Use:

- If you're in the post-menstrual phase and need to rebuild
- If you want a natural source of collagen and minerals
- If you're looking for nourishment that doesn't trigger hunger
- If you're doing a broth-only day to lighten up

FUNCTIONAL BROTHS

35. Warm Broth with Carrot, Celery, and Lemon

A lighter take on classic broth, ideal for moments when you need warmth and cleansing at the same time.

Ingredients
(Serves 1)

- 1 small carrot
- ½ celery stalk
- 1¾ cups water (400 ml)
- juice of ¼ lemon
- 1 pinch of Pink Salt

Instructions

1. Chop the vegetables and simmer in water for 15 minutes.
2. Strain or blend if preferred.
3. Add lemon juice and Pink Salt at the end, stir well, and drink warm.

When to Use:

- If you want a light, digestive version of broth
- If you feel bloated but need something warm
- If you're looking for a calming evening ritual after a busy day
- If you're in your luteal phase and need grounding and balance

VEGETABLE-BASED AND FERMENTED DISHES

36. Warm Salad with Fermented Red Cabbage

A simple yet strategic dish: it combines cooked fiber and live ferments to support digestion and regularity.

Ingredients
(Serves 1)

- ½ cup fermented red cabbage (red sauerkraut)
- 1 small steamed potato
- 1 teaspoon extra virgin olive oil
- 1 pinch of Pink Salt (only if the sauerkraut is not already salted)

Instructions

1. Dice the potato and warm it up slightly.
2. Add the sauerkraut and olive oil.
3. Gently mix everything together and serve warm.

When to Use:

- If you want a gentle introduction to fermented foods
- After antibiotics or during a gut detox
- When you feel bloated but need fiber
- During the follicular phase to reactivate digestion

VEGETABLE-BASED AND FERMENTED DISHES

37. Chickpea Hummus with Cumin and Pink Salt

A versatile spread, rich in plant-based protein and flavor—perfect as a base or balanced snack.

Ingredients
(Serves 1)

- 3.5 oz (about ½ cup) cooked chickpeas
- 1 tablespoon tahini
- ½ teaspoon ground cumin
- Juice of ½ lemon
- 1 pinch of Pink Salt
- Water, as needed, for desired creaminess

Instructions

1. Blend all ingredients until smooth.
2. Slowly add water to adjust the consistency.
3. Serve with raw veggies or whole grain bread.

When to Use:

- When you need a digestible plant-based protein
- If you're looking for a satisfying, non-bloating dish
- During the luteal phase for comfort and stability
- As a functional, sugar-free snack

VEGETABLE-BASED AND FERMENTED DISHES

38. Simplified Homemade Kimchi

A vibrant, living ferment that brings a bold, probiotic-rich touch to any dish.

Ingredients
(Serves 1)

- 1 handful of green or Napa cabbage
- ½ grated carrot
- 1 pinch of chili flakes (optional)
- 1 teaspoon Pink Salt
- 1 teaspoon apple cider vinegar
- Water, as needed

Instructions

1. Mix the vegetables with Pink Salt and let rest for 1 hour.
2. Rinse, then place in a jar with vinegar and enough water to cover.
3. Let ferment at room temperature for 24–48 hours.
4. Store in the fridge.

When to Use:

- To strengthen your gut microbiome with live ferments
- If you're ready for a bold, probiotic flavor
- During an intestinal "reset" phase
- As a flavorful base for any meal

VEGETABLE-BASED AND FERMENTED DISHES

39. Buddha Bowl with Sauerkraut and Toasted Seeds

A complete, balanced bowl combining fiber, probiotics, and healthy fats for a centering meal.

Ingredients
(Serves 1)

- ½ cup cooked brown rice
- 1 handful natural sauerkraut
- ½ avocado
- 1 tablespoon mixed seeds (flax, sunflower, pumpkin)
- 1 teaspoon flaxseed oil
- 1 pinch of Pink Salt

Instructions

1. Build the bowl starting with rice as the base.
2. Add sliced avocado, sauerkraut, and toasted seeds.
3. Drizzle with Pink Salt and flaxseed oil.

When to Use:

- When you want a complete but light meal
- For a balance of fiber, healthy fats, and probiotics
- During the pre-ovulatory phase for regularity
- After an off-balance day when you need to feel centered

VEGETABLE-BASED AND FERMENTED DISHES

40. Stir-Fried Tofu with Spinach and Tamari

A plant-based entrée rich in protein and micronutrients, designed to support your body without weighing it down.

Ingredients
(Serves 1)

- 3.5 oz (about ½ cup) plain tofu
- 1 handful fresh spinach
- 1 teaspoon gluten-free tamari
- 1 teaspoon sesame oil or extra virgin olive oil
- 1 pinch of Pink Salt

Instructions

1. Cube the tofu and stir-fry it in a pan with the oil.
2. Add the spinach and cook until wilted.
3. Add tamari and Pink Salt at the end.
4. Serve warm or at room temperature.

When to Use it:

- When you want to increase protein without using meat
- During the follicular phase for clean energy
- If you're looking for a light yet nutrient-rich dish
- To support gut balance with plant-based protein

SEASONINGS AND DIGESTIVE MIXES

41. Pink Salt & Flaxseed Gomasio

A crunchy, smart seasoning, rich in minerals and healthy fats—perfect to liven up your dishes.

Ingredients
(Serves 1)

- 2 tablespoons flaxseeds
- 1 tablespoon sesame seeds
- 1 teaspoon Pink Salt

Instructions

1. Lightly toast the seeds in a skillet, then blend or grind them with the Pink Salt using a mortar and pestle until you get a fine crumble.
2. Store in an airtight jar.

When to Use it:

- If you want a simple way to get Omega-3s and minerals
- If you're looking for a filling topping for soups or veggies
- If you're in the premenstrual or menstrual phase and feeling bloated
- If you want to boost nutrient absorption without overloading your system

SEASONINGS AND DIGESTIVE MIXES

42. "Digestive" Dressing with Lemon, Olive Oil & Pink Salt

A simple but strategic emulsion that stimulates bile flow and lightens any dish with a single gesture.

Ingredients
(1 serving)

- Juice of ½ lemon
- 1 tablespoon extra virgin olive oil
- 1 pinch Pink Salt

Instructions

1. Whisk all ingredients in a small bowl with a fork.
2. Use as a dressing for raw or cooked vegetables or whole grains.

When to Use it:

- If you feel heavy after lunch or dinner
- If you want to activate bile flow naturally
- If you struggle to digest fats
- If you're easing back into your routine after overindulging

SEASONINGS AND DIGESTIVE MIXES

43. Toasted Seed Mix with Fennel & Cumin

An ancient and powerful ritual: helps reduce bloating, supports digestion, and mindfully closes your meals.

Ingredients
(1 serving - base dose)

- 1 teaspoon fennel seeds
- 1 teaspoon cumin seeds
- 1 pinch Pink Salt

Instructions

1. Lightly toast the seeds in a skillet until they begin to release their aroma.
2. Add the Pink Salt and store in a small jar.
3. Chew slowly at the end of your meal.

When to Use it:

- If you feel bloated or heavy after lunch
- If you tend to have intestinal gas or constipation
- If you want to support digestion naturally
- If you're looking for a mindful end-of-meal ritual that feels like self-care

SEASONINGS AND DIGESTIVE MIXES

44. Yogurt Sauce with Mint & Cucumber

Fresh and creamy—perfect to cool down a spicy dish and support digestion.

Ingredients
(1 serving)

- 2 tablespoons full-fat Greek yogurt
- ¼ grated and squeezed cucumber
- 3 chopped fresh mint leaves
- 1 pinch Pink Salt

Instructions

1. Mix all the ingredients in a bowl until you get a smooth cream.
2. Serve chilled as a side for warm dishes or vegetables.

When to Use it:

- If you want a refreshing, savory digestive treat
- If you're ovulating and need hydrating meals
- If you want to balance the heat of a spicy dish
- If you crave warmth in flavor, but coolness in your body

SEASONINGS AND DIGESTIVE MIXES

45. Tahini Sauce with Garlic & Lemon

Intense, creamy, and functional: a sauce that stimulates digestion and adds depth to your meals.

Ingredients
(1 serving)

- 1 tablespoon tahini
- 1 tablespoon water
- ½ clove garlic, grated
- Juice of ½ lemon
- 1 pinch Pink Salt

Instructions

1. Mix all ingredients until smooth.
2. Add more water only if needed to adjust the texture.
3. Use as a dressing or dip.

When to Use it:

- If you want to stimulate digestion with a bold flavor
- If you're in your luteal phase and need rich yet balanced tastes
- If you're coming out of a flat day and want to revive your plate
- If you're looking for a sauce that encourages mindful chewing

CHAPTER 7
BURN BETTER WITHOUT BURNING OUT

SNACKS THAT ACTIVATE YOUR METABOLISM

46. Activated Almonds with Paprika and Pink Salt

A crunchy, spicy snack that reactivates the metabolism and tames hunger without sugar.

Ingredients
(Serves 1)

- 1 handful (about ¾ oz or 0.7 oz / ~0.75 oz) of raw almonds
- ½ teaspoon sweet or smoked paprika
- 1 pinch of Pink Salt
- Water, as needed for soaking

Instructions

1. Soak the almonds for 6–8 hours (or overnight), then drain and pat dry.
2. Toast them in a skillet with paprika and Pink Salt for 3–4 minutes.

When to Use it:

- When you need a satisfying snack with minimal effort
- During your follicular phase, for activation without stress
- When you want to avoid the blood sugar spikes of sweet snacks
- When you're looking for something warming and rebalancing

SNACKS THAT ACTIVATE YOUR METABOLISM

47. Seed Crackers with Turmeric

Very light, fiber-rich, and flavorful: perfect to calm emotional hunger without triggering cravings.

Ingredients
(Serves 1)

- 1 tablespoon flaxseeds
- 1 tablespoon sunflower seeds
- ½ teaspoon turmeric
- 1 pinch of Pink Salt
- Water, as needed

Instructions

1. Mix the seeds with turmeric, Pink Salt, and just enough water to create a thick mixture.
2. Spread onto parchment paper and bake at 300°F for 20–25 minutes.
3. Let cool and break into pieces.

When to Use:

- When you need a portable, sugar-free snack
- When you crave something savory and functional
- When you're working on stabilizing blood sugar
- When you want to quiet stress-snacking with smart fiber

SNACKS THAT ACTIVATE YOUR METABOLISM

48. "Spicy" Mix with Chili and Pumpkin Seeds

A mini-booster that stimulates the metabolism and supplies zinc to naturally support hormones.

Ingredients
(Serves 1)

- 1 tablespoon pumpkin seeds
- 1 pinch chili powder
- 1 pinch of Pink Salt
- 1 teaspoon extra virgin olive oil

Instructions

1. Lightly toast the seeds in a skillet with olive oil.
2. Remove from heat and add Pink Salt and chili powder.
3. Mix and serve warm or cool.

When to Use:

- When your energy dips mid-afternoon
- When you want a stimulating snack without sugar
- When you're looking for natural hormonal support (thanks to zinc)
- When you need a true reactivating pause

SNACKS THAT ACTIVATE YOUR METABOLISM

49. Baked Kale Chips

Crispy, light, and filling: a great alternative to regular chips, full of fiber and micronutrients.

Ingredients
(Serves 1)

- 3–4 Tuscan kale leaves (aka Lacinato or dinosaur kale)
- 1 teaspoon extra virgin olive oil
- 1 pinch of Pink Salt

Instructions

1. Wash and dry the leaves thoroughly. Remove the center stem and tear into pieces.
2. Toss with olive oil and Pink Salt.
3. Bake at 300°F for 10–12 minutes until crisp.

When to Use:

- When you crave something crunchy but light
- When you want a post-lunch snack that won't reignite hunger
- When you want to support drainage and metabolism
- When you're looking for a healthier chip alternative

SNACKS THAT ACTIVATE YOUR METABOLISM

50. Avocado Lime Mousse

Creamy, just-fatty-enough, refreshing: a smart comfort food that satisfies and nourishes in balance.

Ingredients
(Serves 1)

- ½ ripe avocado
- Juice of ½ lime
- 1 pinch of Pink Salt
- Optional: ½ teaspoon flaxseed oil or hemp seeds

Instructions

1. Mash or blend the avocado with lime juice and Pink Salt until smooth.
2. Add the oil or seeds if you want an extra boost.

When to Use:

- When you feel irritable but constantly hungry
- When you need a source of calming, healthy fats
- During your luteal or premenstrual phase
- When you want a snack that satisfies without tiring you out

SMART RECIPES TO AVOID BLOOD SUGAR SPIKES

51. Chickpea Pancake with Avocado

A savory and satisfying dish that stabilizes blood sugar and supports steady energy without triggering emotional hunger.

Ingredients
(Serves 1)

- 2 tablespoons chickpea flour
- 3 tablespoons water (about 1.7 fl oz)
- A pinch of turmeric and Pink Salt
- ½ ripe avocado

Instructions

1. Mix the flour, water, turmeric, and salt to form a batter.
2. Cook in a non-stick skillet like a pancake.
3. Top with mashed avocado and season with Pink Salt and, if you like, a squeeze of lemon juice.

Recommended when:

- You wake up hungry but want to stay steady for hours
- You want to avoid sweet breakfasts that crash you after 1 hour
- You're in the follicular phase and need a clean, strong base
- You want a versatile recipe, even one you can take on the go

52. Baked Lentil Balls

High in protein and fiber with a low glycemic impact: a smart choice for your main meal.

Ingredients
(serves 1 - makes 3 balls)

- ½ cup cooked lentils
- 1 tablespoon oat flour or chickpea flour
- ½ garlic clove
- Herbs of your choice
- A pinch of Pink Salt

Instructions

1. Blend or mash the lentils with the other ingredients.
2. Shape into small balls, place on parchment paper, and bake at 350°F for 20 minutes.
3. Flip halfway through.

Recommended when:

- You're in the premenstrual phase and want something satisfying without triggering food spirals
- You want to eat "smart carbs" that don't lead to cravings
- You're looking for a lunch or dinner that fills you up without weighing you down
- You're rebalancing after a few days of overindulgence

53. Spiced Pumpkin Cream with Pink Salt

Natural sweetness, warmth, and balance: a soothing cream that doesn't trigger sugar cravings.

Ingredients
(Serves 1)

- ⅔ cup steamed or roasted pumpkin (about 5.3 oz)
- ½ teaspoon cinnamon or mild curry powder
- A pinch of Pink Salt
- Optional: 1 teaspoon coconut oil

Instructions

1. Blend the pumpkin with the spices and salt.
2. Add the coconut oil if you want a richer, more filling texture.
3. Serve warm or at room temperature.

Recommended when:

- You feel nervous hunger in the late afternoon
- You want a calming dish without sugar
- You need a go-to dinner option that's light yet nourishing
- You're in the luteal phase and craving balanced sweetness

SMART RECIPES TO AVOID BLOOD SUGAR SPIKES

54. Hard-Boiled Eggs with Hemp Seeds

A simple, complete combo to fuel you quickly, steadily, and sugar-free.

Ingredients
(Serves 1)

- 2 eggs
- 1 teaspoon shelled hemp seeds
- A pinch of Pink Salt
- Optional: a drizzle of olive oil

Instructions

1. Boil the eggs for 8–9 minutes.
2. Once cooled, peel and slice in half.
3. Sprinkle with hemp seeds and Pink Salt.
4. Add a drizzle of olive oil if you like.

Recommended when:

- You've got a meeting, workout, or long task ahead
- You're in the pre-ovulatory phase and need a clean energy boost
- You skipped a meal and want a smart way to refuel
- You're looking for a protein-rich snack that won't cause an energy crash

SMART RECIPES TO AVOID BLOOD SUGAR SPIKES

55. Protein Wrap with Hummus and Raw Veggies

Crispy, balanced, and satisfying: perfect when you crave something "bready" but steady.

Ingredients
(Serves 1)

- 1 whole grain wrap (preferably protein-rich or legume-based)
- 2 tablespoons hummus
- Raw vegetables to taste (e.g., carrots, arugula, cucumber)
- A pinch of Pink Salt

Instructions

1. Spread the hummus on the wrap, add the veggies, and roll it up.
2. Slice in half for easier handling.

Recommended when:

- You want a "savory but healthy" snack
- You're out and don't want to end up with crackers or pastries
- You need a quick alternative to a sandwich
- You're learning to balance carbs and fats smartly

IDEAS FOR MINI / SEMI-FASTS

56. Liquid Vegetable Cream with Pink Salt

A minimalist, regenerating soup designed to lighten the body without shutting it down—ideal on digestive rest days.

Ingredients
(Serves 1)

- 1 zucchini
- 1 celery stalk
- 1¼ cups of water
- 1 teaspoon raw extra virgin olive oil
- 1 pinch of Pink Salt

Instructions

1. Cook the vegetables in water for 10–12 minutes.
2. Blend until smooth and fluid.
3. Add Pink Salt and olive oil only at the end.
4. Sip slowly, like a thick broth.

When to Use it:

- If you're doing a liquid mini-fast
- If you're in a debloating phase and want something gentle
- If you're experiencing mental hunger but your stomach says "no"
- If you want something warm but as light as water

IDEAS FOR MINI / SEMI-FASTS

57. Warm Water with Pink Salt and Lime Juice

Functional, quick, and effective: a morning activator that jumpstarts digestion and mental clarity.

Ingredients
(Serves 1)

- ¾ cup of warm water
- Juice of ½ lime
- 1 pinch of Pink Salt

Instructions

1. Mix everything in a glass and drink slowly, preferably on an empty stomach in the morning.

When to Use it:

- If you wake up feeling heavy but not hungry
- If you want to naturally support liver function and metabolism
- If you're on a semi-fast and need to replenish electrolytes
- If you want a "lean" version of the morning drink

IDEAS FOR MINI / SEMI-FASTS

58. Lemon & Ginger Infusion

A detox classic enriched with minerals: hydrating and anti-inflammatory, ideal to calm without draining.

Ingredients
(Serves 1)

- ¾ cup of boiling water
- 2 slices of lemon
- 2 slices of fresh ginger
- 1 pinch of Pink Salt

Instructions

1. Boil water and pour it over the lemon and ginger slices.
2. Let steep for 7–8 minutes.
3. Add Pink Salt at the end and drink warm.

When to Use it:

- If you're fasting but want to maintain internal warmth
- If you have cramps, nausea, or acidity
- If you want a soothing evening ritual to reduce inflammation and relax
- If your digestion is slow but you don't want solid food

IDEAS FOR MINI / SEMI-FASTS

59. Mini Evening Vegetable Broth

A warm, light broth that soothes the stomach and closes the day with a sense of peace.

Ingredients
(Serves 1)

- 1 small carrot
- 1 celery stalk
- 1⅔ cups of water
- 1 pinch of Pink Salt
- Optional: fresh herbs (bay leaf, parsley)

Instructions

1. Simmer vegetables in water for 20 minutes.
2. Strain, add Pink Salt, and sip slowly as a calming end-of-day ritual.

When to Use it:

- If you want a liquid dinner that's still comforting
- If you're mentally hungry and want to "close the day"
- If you're in a detox phase and need to restore warmth and minerals
- If your belly feels tight and needs gentle relaxation

IDEAS FOR MINI / SEMI-FASTS

60. Sip of Diluted Kefir with Pink Salt

A fermented, remineralizing drink that supports the microbiome during partial reset days.

Ingredients
(Serves 1)

- ⅓ cup of kefir (preferably homemade or plain)
- ¼ cup of water
- 1 pinch of Pink Salt

Instructions

1. Mix kefir and water in a glass.
2. Add Pink Salt and drink slowly, preferably between solid meals.

When to Use it:

- If you're on a semi-fast and want to nourish your microbiota
- If you're dealing with nervous hunger and want to soothe it gently
- If you want to calm the gut without filling it
- If you need a functional drink—not just something refreshing

CHAPTER 8
FUNCTIONAL PROTEINS: MEAT AND FISH IN THE PINK SALT METHOD

LIGHT FISH TO DEBLOAT AND NOURISH

61. Steamed Mackerel Fillets with Lemon and Pink Salt

Rich in Omega-3s and minerals, this is a light yet strengthening dish, perfect for reducing water retention and regaining clarity.

Ingredients
(1 serving)

- 1 mackerel fillet (fresh or thawed)
- Juice of ½ lemon
- 1 teaspoon extra virgin olive oil
- A generous pinch of Pink Salt

Instructions

1. Steam the fillet for 6–8 minutes.
2. Dress with lemon juice, Pink Salt, and olive oil.
3. Serve warm with leafy greens or zucchini.

When to Use it:

- If you're feeling bloated and mentally foggy
- If you want a protein-rich meal that won't weigh you down
- If you're in your follicular phase or after a detox day
- If your liver needs support and you're aiming to reduce inflammation

> LIGHT FISH TO DEBLOAT AND NOURISH

62. Baked Salmon with Herbs and Orange Zest

Rich, aromatic, and hormone-friendly: a deeply nourishing recipe that won't cause inflammation.

Ingredients
(1 serving)

- 1 salmon fillet (about 4–5 oz)
- Grated zest of an organic orange
- Fresh thyme or rosemary
- A pinch of Pink Salt

Instructions

1. Place the salmon on parchment paper.
2. Add herbs, orange zest, and Pink Salt.
3. Bake at 350°F for 15 minutes.
4. Serve with bitter greens or a fresh salad.

When to Use it:

- If you're in the luteal phase and want to nourish without bloating
- If you need a dish that "grounds" you
- If you're looking to support hormone regulation
- If you want something flavorful yet anti-inflammatory

LIGHT FISH TO DEBLOAT AND NOURISH

63. Cod Soup with Ginger and Sweet Potatoes

Gentle yet rich, perfect for those who are genuinely hungry but have sensitive stomachs.

Ingredients
(1 serving)

- 1 cod fillet (fresh or frozen)
- 1 small sweet potato
- ½ inch fresh ginger root
- 1 ¼ cups (10 fl oz) water
- A pinch of Pink Salt

Instructions

1. Dice the sweet potato and cook with the ginger in water for 10 minutes.
2. Add the cod and cook for another 5 minutes.
3. Salt at the end and serve hot.

When to Use it:

- If you feel drained or disconnected
- If you need warming digestion and balanced sweetness
- If you're premenstrual and experiencing constant hunger
- If you want a one-bowl meal that also supports detox

LIGHT FISH TO DEBLOAT AND NOURISH

64. Tuna Tartare with Avocado, Lime, and a Pinch of Pink Salt

Fresh, rich in healthy fats, and full of vitality: ideal for days when you're hungry but still crave lightness.

Ingredients
(1 serving)

- 3–3.5 oz sushi-grade raw tuna
- ½ avocado
- Juice of ½ lime
- A pinch of Pink Salt
- Optional: a few drops of tamari or sesame sauce

Instructions

1. Dice the tuna and avocado.
2. Season with lime juice, Pink Salt, and any optional extras.
3. Let marinate for 5 minutes before serving.

When to Use it:

- If you're ovulating and seeking clean energy
- If you need a meal that's fresh yet satisfying
- If it's a hot or inflammatory day
- If you want to boost your metabolism with a raw, functional dish

LIGHT FISH TO DEBLOAT AND NOURISH

65. Warm Salad with Marinated Anchovies, Fennel, and Pumpkin Seeds

Debloating, mineral-rich, and hormone-balancing: a smart dish for your belly and your cycle.

Ingredients
(1 serving)

- 3–4 marinated anchovy fillets (sugar-free)
- ½ fennel bulb, thinly sliced
- 1 teaspoon pumpkin seeds
- 1 teaspoon extra virgin olive oil
- A pinch of Pink Salt

Instructions

1. Slice the fennel and blanch it in hot water for 2 minutes (or use raw if preferred).
2. Add anchovies, toasted seeds, and Pink Salt.
3. Serve warm or at room temperature.

When to Use it:

- If you feel bloated but want something complete
- If you want a dish that supports gut health and your cycle
- If you're in the pre-ovulatory phase and want structured lightness
- If you're hungry but don't want to feel heavy

LIGHT MEATS TO SUPPORT HORMONES AND METABOLISM

66. Sweet Curry Chicken with Coconut Milk and Pink Salt

Comforting and calming—perfect when you need warmth, nourishment, and a touch of balancing exotic flavor.

Ingredients
(Serves 1)

- 4 oz diced chicken breast
- ⅓ cup light coconut milk
- ½ tsp mild curry powder
- 1 pinch of Pink Salt
- 1 tsp extra virgin olive oil

Instructions

1. Cook the chicken in olive oil for 2–3 minutes, then add the curry powder and coconut milk.
2. Let simmer for 8–10 minutes.
3. Add the Pink Salt at the end.
4. Serve with vegetables or brown rice.

Suggested for you when:

- You're in the luteal phase and want to support progesterone and mood
- You're craving a complete, comforting meal
- You need a protein-rich dish without overdoing it
- You're having an off day and want to recenter yourself

LIGHT MEATS TO SUPPORT HORMONES AND METABOLISM

67. Turkey Strips with Rosemary and Lemon Zest

Light, aromatic, and easy to digest—a dish that tones without weighing you down.

Ingredients
(Serves 1)

- 4 oz thinly sliced turkey breast
- 1 tsp extra virgin olive oil
- Fresh chopped rosemary
- Grated zest of an organic lemon
- 1 pinch of Pink Salt

Instructions

1. Heat the oil in a skillet, add the turkey, and cook for 4–5 minutes.
2. Season with rosemary, lemon zest, and Pink Salt.
3. Serve with a light side dish.

Suggested for you when:

- You're in the follicular phase and want clean energy
- You're looking for a light but regenerating meal
- You want a quick alternative to plant-based proteins
- You're on a low-glycemic day and want to stay balanced

LIGHT MEATS TO SUPPORT HORMONES AND METABOLISM

68. Bone Broth with Pink Salt, Carrots, and Ginger

A mineral-rich, nourishing comfort—perfect for calming, restoring, and deeply rebalancing.

Ingredients
(Serves 1)

- 1 ¼ cups bone broth (beef or chicken, homemade or store-bought)
- 1 sliced carrot
- ½ inch fresh ginger, peeled and sliced
- 1 pinch of Pink Salt

Instructions

1. Warm the broth with the carrot and ginger.
2. Let simmer for 10 minutes.
3. Add Pink Salt at the end and sip slowly.

Suggested for you when:

- You're in the post-menstrual phase and need to rebuild
- You want a liquid dish that still feels complete
- You want to soothe your gut and nervous system
- You're detoxing but don't want to feel depleted

LIGHT MEATS TO SUPPORT HORMONES AND METABOLISM

69. Chicken Breast Salad with Green Apple and Red Cabbage

Crunchy, detoxifying, and balanced—a perfect dish if you want to debloat without sacrificing fullness.

Ingredients
(Serves 1)

- 3.5 oz cooked chicken breast, cut into strips
- ½ green apple, thinly sliced
- 1 handful raw red cabbage, shredded
- 1 tsp extra virgin olive oil
- 1 pinch of Pink Salt

Instructions

1. Combine all ingredients in a bowl.
2. Dress with olive oil and Pink Salt, and let rest for 5 minutes before eating.

Suggested for you when:

- You want lightness and cleansing with protein balance
- You're in the ovulatory phase and need a detox boost
- You need a quick lunch that keeps you full
- You feel bloated but still hungry

LIGHT MEATS TO SUPPORT HORMONES AND METABOLISM

70. Baked Lean Meatballs with Sweet Spices

Flavorful yet light, calming and stabilizing—a hormonally smart comfort food.

Ingredients
(serves 1 - makes 3-4 meatballs)

- 3.5 oz lean ground meat (chicken or turkey)
- 1 tsp cumin seeds
- ½ tsp sweet paprika
- 1 pinch cinnamon
- 1 pinch of Pink Salt

Instructions

1. Mix all ingredients.
2. Form into meatballs and bake at 350°F for 15–20 minutes.
3. Serve with cooked or raw vegetables.

Suggested for you when:

- You're dealing with emotional hunger but want to stay balanced
- You're in the premenstrual phase and need warmth and grounding
- You're coming out of a chaotic stretch and want to recenter
- You want a nourishing yet light meal

CHAPTER 9
EMOTIONAL RECIPES: WHEN YOU'RE CRAVING SOMETHING

COMFORT SNACKS WITHOUT SABOTAGE

71. Dark Chocolate with Walnuts and Pink Salt

An intense, instant comfort—perfect for calming cravings without triggering hunger.

Ingredients
(for 1 serving)

- 2 squares of 90% dark chocolate
- 1 teaspoon coarsely chopped walnuts
- A pinch of Pink Salt

Instructions

1. Lightly melt the chocolate using a double boiler or microwave (optional).
2. Sprinkle with walnuts and Pink Salt.
3. Let rest for 2 minutes or enjoy immediately.

When to Use it:

- When a sweet craving hits and you want to stay grounded
- During PMS when you need deep satisfaction
- When you want a moment of pleasure that brings you back into your body
- When you need a craving-proof pause ritual

COMFORT SNACKS WITHOUT SABOTAGE

72. Coconut Pink Salt Popcorn

Crunchy, light, and filling—perfect for when you want to snack without wrecking everything.

Ingredients
(for 1 serving)

- 2 tablespoons popcorn kernels
- 1 teaspoon coconut oil
- A generous pinch of Pink Salt

Instructions

1. Heat the coconut oil in a small pot.
2. Add the kernels and cover with a lid.
3. Let them pop until it stops.
4. Add Pink Salt and mix well.

When to Use it:

- For a movie snack that won't disrupt your reset
- When you're craving something salty and crunchy
- During PMS for volume without heaviness
- When you need to keep your mind busy with a smart snack

COMFORT SNACKS WITHOUT SABOTAGE

73. Apple Chips with Cinnamon

Sweet, light, and craving-proof—perfect for evening snack attacks or anxious afternoons.

Ingredients
(for 1 serving)

- 1 apple (preferably with thin skin)
- ½ teaspoon ground cinnamon
- Optional: a pinch of Pink Salt

Instructions

1. Slice the apple thinly.
2. Dust with cinnamon (and Pink Salt if you want a salty note).
3. Bake at 210°F for 1 hour, or air-fry for 20–25 minutes.

When to Use it:

- When you need a sugar-free sweet
- To satisfy your taste buds without sparking cravings
- On slow days when you need gentle energy
- For a light, aromatic ritual

COMFORT SNACKS WITHOUT SABOTAGE

74. Frozen Banana Cocoa Mousse

A natural, creamy, and satisfying ice cream that won't disrupt digestion or awaken hunger.

Ingredients
(for 1 serving)

- 1 ripe banana, sliced and frozen
- 1 teaspoon unsweetened cocoa powder
- A pinch of Pink Salt
- Optional: ½ teaspoon almond butter

Instructions

1. Blend the frozen banana with cocoa and Pink Salt until smooth and creamy.
2. Add almond butter for extra creaminess and satiety.

When to Use it:

- After dinner when you want a sweet treat without sugar
- For a functional dessert to savor slowly
- On emotional days when you need clean relief
- When you want to practice enjoying without overdoing

COMFORT SNACKS WITHOUT SABOTAGE

75. Oat & Seed Mini Cookies

Crunchy, filling, and fiber-rich—these tame hunger and give a "homemade" feeling that calms the mind.

Ingredients

(for 1 serving - makes 3 cookies)

- 2 tablespoons rolled oats
- 1 teaspoon mixed seeds (sunflower, flax, pumpkin)
- 1 teaspoon almond butter or tahini
- 1 teaspoon water
- A pinch of Pink Salt

Instructions

1. Mix all ingredients into a firm dough.
2. Shape into 3 small discs and bake at 350°F for 10–12 minutes.

When to Use it:

- When you need a snack that helps you feel "back on track"
- During PMS when you want a cookie without guilt
- When you need to soothe chewing anxiety
- For an on-the-go snack, even on your most unpredictable days

ANTI-CRAVING SWEETS

76. Energy Bites with Dates, Cocoa, and Pink Salt

Small, intense, satisfying: perfect when you're craving something sweet and substantial.

Ingredients
(serves 1 - makes 2 bites)

- 2 soft dates
- 1 teaspoon unsweetened cocoa powder
- 1 teaspoon chopped almonds or almond flour
- A pinch of Pink Salt

Instructions

1. Blend the dates with the cocoa and almonds.
2. Form into two small balls and roll them in either cocoa or Pink Salt.
3. Store in the fridge or enjoy right away.

When to Use it:

- If you're in your premenstrual phase and craving deep sweetness
- If you want something to enjoy slowly and mindfully
- If you're looking for an alternative to processed chocolates
- If you're working on cravings but don't want to give up flavor

ANTI-CRAVING SWEETS

77. Almond and Seed Bars

Crunchy, dense, and balanced: a sweet snack that stabilizes rather than spikes.

Ingredients
(serves 1 - makes 1 bar)

- 1 tablespoon chopped almonds
- 1 teaspoon pumpkin or sunflower seeds
- 1 teaspoon honey (or coconut syrup)
- A pinch of Pink Salt

Instructions

1. Mix everything together and press into a strip on parchment paper.
2. Let chill in the fridge for at least 1 hour.
3. For extra crunch, you can also bake it for 10 minutes at 320°F.

When to Use it:

- If you want a sweet snack that doesn't cause an energy crash
- If you need a portable, stable, and satisfying treat
- If you're having a mentally demanding day and want to stay centered
- If you're looking for something that helps you stay connected to your body

ANTI-CRAVING SWEETS

78. Apple Crumble with Almond Flour

An oven-baked comfort that smells like home and satisfies sweet cravings with fiber and healthy fats.

Ingredients
(Serves 1)

- 1 small apple, diced
- 1 tablespoon almond flour
- ½ teaspoon cinnamon
- A pinch of Pink Salt
- Optional: 1 teaspoon coconut oil or ghee

Instructions

1. Place the apple in a small baking dish.
2. Mix the almond flour with cinnamon, salt, and oil (if using).
3. Sprinkle over the apple and bake at 350°F for 15 minutes.
4. Enjoy warm.

When to Use it:

- If you're craving a warm dessert but want to stay on track
- If you're in your premenstrual phase and need comfort and warmth
- If you want an evening ritual that soothes instead of stimulates
- If you need sweetness without free sugars

ANTI-CRAVING SWEETS

79. Greek Yogurt with Honey, Cinnamon, and Pink Salt

Quick, balanced, and satisfying: a protein-packed dessert that soothes cravings.

Ingredients
(Serves 1)

- 3 tablespoons full-fat Greek yogurt
- 1 teaspoon raw honey
- ½ teaspoon cinnamon
- A pinch of Pink Salt

Instructions

1. Mix everything in a small bowl and enjoy slowly, even with a small spoon to increase mindfulness.

When to Use it:

- If you crave something sweet after lunch
- If you want satiety with just a few real ingredients
- If you're under stress and want regulating sweetness
- If you want to avoid heavy desserts without giving up taste

ANTI-CRAVING SWEETS

80. Chia Seed Pudding with Berries

Creamy, fresh, and functional: a dessert that nourishes gut flora and calms sweet impulses.

Ingredients
(Serves 1)

- 1 tablespoon chia seeds
- ⅓ cup (approx. 3.4 oz) unsweetened plant-based milk
- 1 handful of berries (fresh or frozen)
- A pinch of Pink Salt
- Optional: a few drops of vanilla extract

Instructions

1. Mix the chia seeds with the plant milk and Pink Salt.
2. Let rest in the fridge for at least 1 hour.
3. Add berries on top and stir before eating.

When to Use it:

- If you're in your post-cycle phase and want to restart with clean energy
- If you want a dessert that also supports your gut health
- If you're looking for a sweet treat to take to work or on the go
- If you're creating new, intimate food rituals

LIGHT COMFORT FOODS

81. Sweet Potato Mash with Almond Milk

A soft, naturally sweet, and balancing dish: it soothes the nervous system and nourishes gently.

Ingredients
(Serves 1)

- 1 small sweet potato
- 3 tablespoons unsweetened almond milk
- 1 pinch Pink Salt
- Optional: a dash of nutmeg or cinnamon

Instructions

1. Steam or boil the sweet potato.
2. Mash it with the warm almond milk and add Pink Salt and spices.
3. Mix until smooth and creamy.

When to try it:

- When you're tired, emotional, and craving softness
- When you want a warm dish that calms without weighing you down
- When you're in the premenstrual phase or having a "low" day
- When you need real comfort food that's still balanced

LIGHT COMFORT FOODS

82. Light Risotto with Vegetable Broth and Lemon

A simple, fragrant dish that warms the stomach and supports easy digestion.

Ingredients
(Serves 1)

- 3 tablespoons brown or semi-polished rice
- 1 ¼ cups (about 10 fl oz) light vegetable broth
- Zest and juice of ¼ lemon
- 1 teaspoon extra virgin olive oil
- 1 pinch Pink Salt

Instructions

1. Cook the rice in the broth with a pinch of salt.
2. Once fully cooked, stir in the lemon zest, juice, and raw olive oil.
3. Mix well and serve warm.

When to try it:

- When you're emotionally hungry but want to stay grounded
- When you want something warm without the bloat
- During your post-cycle or detox day
- When you need a "patient," rebalancing meal

LIGHT COMFORT FOODS

83. Whole Wheat Pasta with Zucchini Cream

Green, creamy, and satisfying: a pasta dish that comforts without heaviness.

Ingredients
(Serves 1)

- 2–2.5 oz (about ⅓ cup) whole wheat pasta (preferably spelt or buckwheat)
- 1 small zucchini
- 1 teaspoon extra virgin olive oil
- 1 pinch Pink Salt
- Optional: a few basil or mint leaves

Instructions

1. Cook the pasta. Meanwhile, steam the zucchini and blend it with oil, salt, and herbs until creamy.
2. Toss the pasta with the zucchini cream.

When to try it:

- When you're craving pasta but want easy digestion
- When you're rebalancing after an irregular period
- When you feel light but hungry
- During ovulation, when you need clean energy

LIGHT COMFORT FOODS

84. Miso Soup with Tofu

A liquid, nourishing, probiotic-rich dish, perfect for a calming evening reset.

Ingredients
(Serves 1)

- 1 teaspoon unpasteurized miso
- ⅔ cup (5 fl oz) warm water (not boiling)
- 2 oz tofu, cubed
- A handful of fresh spinach or seaweed
- 1 pinch Pink Salt (only if miso is mild)

Instructions

1. Heat the water (do not boil).
2. Dissolve the miso, then add tofu and spinach.
3. Let simmer gently for 2–3 minutes and serve.

When to try it:

- When you want a light yet nourishing dinner
- When your gut needs rebalancing
- When you want something warm that doesn't trigger cravings
- When you want to feel clean and centered before bed

LIGHT COMFORT FOODS

85. Polenta with Sautéed Tuscan Kale

A plant-based, mineral-rich comfort food that grounds you without weighing you down.

Ingredients
(Serves 1)

- 3 tablespoons instant cornmeal (polenta)
- A handful of sautéed Tuscan kale (also known as lacinato kale or dinosaur kale)
- 1 teaspoon extra virgin olive oil
- 1 pinch Pink Salt

Instructions

1. Prepare the polenta according to package directions, adding Pink Salt.
2. In a pan, sauté the kale with a small amount of olive oil and a splash of water.
3. Serve over the hot polenta.

When to try it:

- When you're genuinely hungry but want a meal that grounds you
- During the premenstrual phase or emotionally intense days
- When you want to calm and anchor yourself through food
- When you need something warming that won't inflame

CHAPTER 10
FEMALE SUPPORT

CYCLE PHASES AND FOODS THAT HELP

86. Pre-Ovulation Smoothie with Maca and Berries

Energizing and antioxidant-rich, this smoothie helps the body perform at its best during the peak of hormonal activation.

Ingredients

- 1 handful of berries
- ½ banana
- 1 teaspoon maca powder
- ⅓ cup (about 3.4 fl oz) water or plant-based milk
- 1 pinch of Pink Salt

Instructions

1. Blend everything until smooth and creamy.
2. Sip slowly.

When to Use It:

- If you're in the days before ovulation
- If you want to support libido, energy, and focus
- If you need a boost that won't crash you afterward
- If you're looking for a gesture that centers you

CYCLE PHASES AND FOODS THAT HELP

87. Pumpkin Cream for PMS

Sweet, calming, and regulating: ideal for managing hunger, anxiety, and sugar cravings.

Ingredients

- ⅔ cup (about 5.3 oz) steamed pumpkin
- 1 teaspoon cinnamon
- 1 teaspoon coconut oil
- 1 pinch of Pink Salt

Instructions

1. Blend everything until smooth and creamy.
2. Warm it up if desired.

When to Use It:

- If you're in the luteal phase and experiencing mental hunger
- If you want a snack that comforts without sabotaging
- If you need sweetness that regulates
- If you want a soothing evening ritual without triggering cravings

CYCLE PHASES AND FOODS THAT HELP

88. Black Rice with Veggies for Post-Cycle Recovery

Rich in iron, minerals, and fiber: perfect for rebuilding and restoring balance.

Ingredients

- 3 tablespoons cooked black rice
- Diced seasonal vegetables
- 1 teaspoon extra virgin olive oil
- 1 pinch of Pink Salt

Instructions

1. Cook the vegetables and lightly sauté them with the rice and oil.
2. Add Pink Salt at the end.

When to Use It:

- If you're in the days after your period and need reinforcement
- If you want a "tonic" dish that's still easy to digest
- If you're avoiding sugar spikes without overloading on protein
- If you feel a mix of hunger and fatigue

CYCLE PHASES AND FOODS THAT HELP

89. Almond Milk with Saffron for Mood Support

A light and liquid ritual, ideal for supporting your mood during hormonal lows.

Ingredients

- ⅔ cup (about 5 fl oz) unsweetened almond milk
- 2 strands of saffron
- 1 pinch of Pink Salt
- Optional: ½ teaspoon honey

Instructions

1. Warm the almond milk (without boiling), add saffron, salt, and honey.
2. Sip slowly.

When to Use It:

- If you're in a "down" phase and feeling low
- If you want a gesture that supports hormones as well as emotions
- If you need a quiet moment to yourself
- If you're dealing with post-estrogen drop or end-of-cycle slump

CYCLE PHASES AND FOODS THAT HELP

90. Pink Broth with Cabbage and Pink Salt

Mineral-rich, draining, and stabilizing: perfect for de-bloating and nourishing during the most delicate phases.

Ingredients

- 1 leaf red cabbage
- 1 carrot
- 1¾ cups (about 13.5 fl oz) water
- 1 pinch of Pink Salt

Instructions

1. Cook everything for 15 minutes.
2. Strain, add salt, and sip slowly.

When to Use It:

- If you're on your period and feeling bloated and depleted
- If you want warmth and minerals without solid food
- If you're seeking a therapeutic liquid ritual
- If you want to de-bloat without dehydrating

RECIPES FOR OVULATION, MENSTRUATION, AND PREMENSTRUAL PHASE

91. Spinach and Pumpkin Seed Frittata

A simple and functional recipe to support iron, progesterone, and metabolism.

Ingredients

- 2 eggs
- 1 handful of spinach
- 1 teaspoon pumpkin seeds
- 1 pinch of Pink Salt

Instructions

1. Cook the spinach, then mix with the beaten eggs, seeds, and salt.
2. Cook in a skillet.

Recommended when:

- You're ovulating or in the premenstrual phase
- You need a quick but filling breakfast or lunch
- You want hormonal stability with minimal ingredients
- You're looking to support your cycle naturally through food

RECIPES FOR OVULATION, MENSTRUATION, AND PREMENSTRUAL PHASE

92. Cyclical Red Lentil Soup

A thick, nourishing, and calming soup: it supports your cycle, digestion, and mood all at once.

Ingredients

- 2 tablespoons red split lentils
- 1 carrot
- ½ onion
- 1¾ cups water (approx. 14 fl oz)
- 1 pinch of Pink Salt

Instructions

1. Cook all ingredients in water for 20–25 minutes.
2. Blend or leave chunky. Add Pink Salt at the end.

Recommended when:

- You're on your period and need deep nourishment
- You want a dish that satisfies without weighing you down
- You're craving warm, soft proteins
- You want digestive regularity and emotional balance

RECIPES FOR OVULATION, MENSTRUATION, AND PREMENSTRUAL PHASE

93. Sage and Lemon Tea for Day 1

An infusion that soothes cramps, supports the liver, and gently helps your body let go.

Ingredients

- ¾ cup boiling water (approx. 6.8 fl oz)
- 3 sage leaves
- Juice of ¼ lemon
- 1 pinch of Pink Salt

Instructions

1. Let steep for 7 minutes, strain, and drink warm.

Recommended when:

- It's Day 1 of your period and you feel tired or tense
- You want a ritual that opens and supports your body
- You're looking for a real pause that reaches deep into your lower belly
- You want to nourish the most inward phase of your cycle

RECIPES FOR OVULATION, MENSTRUATION, AND PREMENSTRUAL PHASE

94. Lemon and Ginger Risotto (Follicular Phase)

Light, activating, and digestive: perfect to restart with energy after your period.

Ingredients

- 3 tablespoons brown rice
- 1 small piece of fresh ginger
- Lemon zest
- 1¼ cups vegetable broth (approx. 10 fl oz)
- 1 pinch of Pink Salt

Instructions

1. Cook the rice in the broth with ginger and salt.
2. Add the lemon zest at the end of cooking.

Recommended when:

- You want fresh, steady energy
- You're coming out of your cycle and want a good reset
- You're looking for a clean yet stimulating meal
- You want to feel light but grounded

RECIPES FOR OVULATION, MENSTRUATION, AND PREMENSTRUAL PHASE

95. Oat and Banana Muffin (Luteal Phase)

Sweet, soft, and functional: satisfies cravings and gently supports your energy dip.

Ingredients

- ½ ripe banana
- 2 tablespoons rolled oats
- 1 teaspoon coconut oil
- 1 pinch of Pink Salt
- 1 teaspoon water

Instructions

1. Mix all ingredients, pour into a small muffin mold, and bake at 350°F for 12–15 minutes.

Recommended when:

- You're in your premenstrual phase and want a treat that doesn't send you spiraling
- You want a functional way to use up a banana
- You need a portable, anti-craving snack
- You want to comfort yourself without disconnecting

96. Day 1 Drink: Pink Salt + Lemon + Honey

Replenishing and soothing: a drink calibrated for the first day of your cycle.

Ingredients

- 7 oz warm water
- Juice of ½ lemon
- 1 tsp raw honey
- A pinch of Pink Salt

Instructions

1. Mix everything together and sip slowly in the morning.

Recommended when:

- You feel drained or low-energy
- You want to gently replenish
- You want to start your cycle with care and presence
- You're looking for a simple yet powerful ritual

PINK SALT AND HORMONES: HOW TO ADAPT IT TO YOUR RHYTHMS

97. Calming Mix with Warm Water and Salted Chamomile

Sedative, digestive, and hydrating: the perfect combo for tough evenings.

Ingredients

- 1 chamomile tea bag
- 7 oz hot water
- A pinch of Pink Salt

Instructions

1. Brew the tea, add Pink Salt, and drink warm, slowly.

Recommended when:

- You feel tension and bloating at the same time
- You want to sleep without poor digestion
- You're in the luteal phase and need to decompress
- You're looking for a true end-of-day gesture

PINK SALT AND HORMONES: HOW TO ADAPT IT TO YOUR RHYTHMS

98. Morning Ritual with Saline Water and Maca

A gentle hormonal activator, perfect for starting the day in tune with the female body.

Ingredients

- 7 oz warm water
- ½ tsp maca powder
- A pinch of Pink Salt
- Optional: juice of ¼ lemon

Instructions

1. Mix all ingredients and drink on a semi-empty stomach in the morning.

Recommended when:

- You want to signal vitality to your hormones
- You're in pre-ovulation and want to support energy and libido
- You're looking for a functional alternative to coffee
- You want to start your day with a conscious boost

99. Pink Water with Hibiscus and Flaxseeds

Hydrating, mineralizing, and feminine: perfect for sipping throughout your cycle.

Ingredients

- 8.5 oz still water
- 1 tsp dried hibiscus flowers
- 1 tsp flaxseeds (soaked)
- A pinch of Pink Salt

Instructions

1. Prepare a hibiscus infusion, let it cool, add the flaxseeds (with their gel) and salt.
2. Drink cold or at room temperature.

Recommended when:

- You're in the menstrual phase and want to support digestion
- You need smart hydration
- You're looking for an anti-inflammatory, mineral-rich ritual
- You want to carry a drink "for your feminine self"

100. Evening Tonic with Apple Cider Vinegar and a Pinch of Pink Salt

A digestive, alkalizing, and calming tonic to end the day in your body.

Ingredients

- 7 oz warm water
- 1 tsp raw unfiltered apple cider vinegar
- A pinch of Pink Salt

Instructions

1. Mix everything and drink slowly, at least 30 minutes before bed.

Recommended when:

- You want to rebalance your gut at the end of the day
- You feel bloated or heavy and want to decompress
- You're looking for a sugar-free evening ritual
- You're winding down from a demanding day and want to return to yourself

CHAPTER 11
BONUS RECIPES

BONUS: "WANT TO TRY SOMETHING NEW?"

101. Golden Kefir with Pink Salt and Fresh Ginger

A probiotic and anti-inflammatory drink, perfect for calming the stomach and nervous system.

Ingredients
(Serves 1)

- ⅔ cup (about 5 fl oz) plain kefir
- ½ inch fresh ginger, grated
- ½ teaspoon turmeric
- A pinch of Pink Salt
- Optional: ½ teaspoon honey or cinnamon

Instructions

1. Mix all ingredients in a cup.
2. If desired, gently warm the kefir (no hotter than 104°F) to make it lukewarm.
3. Sip slowly, preferably in the evening.

When to Use it:

- When you feel bloated or have intestinal tension
- When you want an evening ritual to relax and nourish your gut
- When you're in PMS or having "heavy" days
- When you're looking for a functional, cozy post-dinner treat

BONUS: "WANT TO TRY SOMETHING NEW?"

102. Purple Beet & Tahini Hummus with Pink Salt

Colorful, mineral-rich, and full of plant-based iron—a perfect spread for bread, veggies, or even eaten by the spoonful.

Ingredients

- ½ cup cooked chickpeas
- ½ medium cooked beet
- 1 tablespoon tahini
- Juice of ½ lemon
- A pinch of Pink Salt

Instructions

1. Blend all ingredients until smooth.
2. Add a tablespoon of water if needed to adjust consistency.
3. Store in the fridge for up to 3 days.

When to Use it:

- During your period when you need iron and vibrant color
- When you want a filling spread that doesn't cause bloating
- When you're tired of standard hummus
- When you want a dish that looks good and feels good

BONUS: "WANT TO TRY SOMETHING NEW?"

103. Baked Zucchini Chips with Smoked Paprika and Pink Salt

Crispy and light—perfect for replacing processed snacks without sacrificing flavor.

Ingredients

- 1 medium zucchini
- 1 teaspoon extra virgin olive oil
- ½ teaspoon smoked paprika
- A pinch of Pink Salt

Instructions

1. Slice zucchini into thin rounds.
2. Toss with oil, paprika, and Pink Salt.
3. Bake at 320°F for 20–25 minutes on parchment paper until crispy.

When to Use it:

- When you want a crunchy snack without derailing everything
- When you're in PMS and craving something salty
- When you need a satisfying afternoon treat
- When you're looking for a healthy alternative to chips

> BONUS: "WANT TO TRY SOMETHING NEW?"

104. "Calm and Clarity" Herbal Infusion with Lavender, Lemon & Pink Salt

A soothing evening ritual to release tension, rebalance, and feel grounded.

Ingredients

- 1 teaspoon dried lavender flowers
- 1 lemon slice
- ¾ cup (about 6.5 fl oz) boiling water
- A pinch of Pink Salt

Instructions

1. Steep lavender and lemon in boiling water for 7–8 minutes.
2. Add Pink Salt at the end and drink warm.

When to Use it:

- When your head feels heavy and your stomach feels tight
- When you're premenstrual or in a low-energy day
- When you need to slow down without turning to food
- When you want to end the day with an intentional act

BONUS: "WANT TO TRY SOMETHING NEW?"

105. Digestive Smoothie with Green Apple, Cucumber, Mint & Pink Salt

Refreshing, alkalizing, and detoxifying—a drink to de-bloat and refresh both body and mind.

Ingredients

- ½ green apple
- ½ cucumber
- 3 fresh mint leaves
- ⅓–½ cup water
- A pinch of Pink Salt

Instructions

1. Blend all ingredients until smooth.
2. Drink immediately, chilled or at room temperature.

When to Use it:

- When you're feeling bloated or overheated
- When you want a light, refreshing post-workout drink
- When you're ovulating and need a detox boost
- When you're craving something that makes you feel "clean"

> BONUS: "WANT TO TRY SOMETHING NEW?"

106. Scrambled Eggs with Turmeric, Baby Spinach, and Pink Salt

A savory, anti-inflammatory, and satisfying breakfast that stabilizes you and provides clean energy.

Ingredients

- 2 eggs
- 1 handful of baby spinach
- ½ teaspoon turmeric
- 1 pinch of Pink Salt
- 1 teaspoon extra virgin olive oil

Instructions

1. Beat the eggs with turmeric and Pink Salt.
2. Cook in a skillet with the oil, add the spinach, and scramble until done.

When to Use it:

- If you want to start your day strong without energy spikes
- If you're in your pre-ovulation phase or want to support liver function
- If you're feeling emotionally hungry and need grounding
- If you want a savory breakfast without bread or cheese

> BONUS: "WANT TO TRY SOMETHING NEW?"

107. Warm Plant-Based Milk with Vanilla, Pink Salt, and Raw Cacao

An evening comfort drink that satisfies cravings without overstimulation.

Ingredients

- ½ cup (about 5 oz) plant-based milk (almond or oat)
- ½ teaspoon raw cacao powder
- 2 drops natural vanilla extract
- 1 pinch of Pink Salt

Instructions

1. Warm the milk (do not boil), add cacao, vanilla, and Pink Salt.
2. Stir and sip slowly.

When to Use it:

- If you're craving something sweet but want to stay balanced
- If you're in your premenstrual phase and want to avoid real chocolate
- If you're looking for a calming nighttime ritual
- If you want to treat yourself without sugar

BONUS: "WANT TO TRY SOMETHING NEW?"

108. Warm Apple and Celery Soup with Pink Salt

Yes, fruit can be detoxifying: this soup is debloating, original, and surprisingly balanced.

Ingredients

- ½ green apple
- 1 stalk of celery
- ¾ cup (about 6.75 oz) water
- 1 pinch of Pink Salt

Instructions

1. Chop the apple and celery, cook in water for 10 minutes.
2. Blend everything, add Pink Salt, and serve warm.

When to Use it:

- If you want to debloat without typical vegetables
- If your stomach feels off and you want something fresh yet warm
- If you're coming off a heavy day and need a reset
- If you're in the follicular phase or post-party

BONUS: "WANT TO TRY SOMETHING NEW?"

109. Basmati Rice with Lemon and Mustard Seeds with Pink Salt

Fragrant, digestible, and flavorful: the perfect base for light but nourishing days.

Ingredients

- 3 tablespoons cooked basmati rice
- Juice and zest of ¼ lemon
- ½ teaspoon mustard seeds
- 1 teaspoon extra virgin olive oil
- 1 pinch of Pink Salt

Instructions

1. Heat the oil in a pan and let the mustard seeds pop.
2. Add the rice, then the lemon juice and zest, and Pink Salt.
3. Stir-fry for a minute and serve.

When to Use it:

- If you're having a sensitive digestion day
- If you want a light meal that's not boring
- If you're in your follicular phase or recovering from an indulgence
- If you need mental energy without bloating

BONUS: "WANT TO TRY SOMETHING NEW?"

110. Avocado and Yogurt Sauce with Pink Salt and Lime Juice

Creamy, tangy, rebalancing: perfect as a spread or to complement whatever's on your plate.

Ingredients

- ½ avocado
- 1 tablespoon full-fat Greek yogurt
- Juice of ¼ lime
- 1 pinch of Pink Salt

Instructions

1. Blend or mash everything until smooth.
2. Serve with vegetables, grains, or rye bread.

When to Use it:

- If you're looking for a functional, filling topping
- If you're ovulating and need something fresh and nutrient-dense
- If you want to add creaminess to your detox meals
- If you want a lighter alternative to cheese or heavier sauces

PART III
YOUR NEW BALANCE

CHAPTER 12
REDISCOVER YOURSELF

How to Create Your Functional Week

The Pink Salt Method isn't a strict diet to follow to the letter. It's a flexible lifestyle you can adapt to your rhythms—and your curveballs.

In this chapter, you'll learn how to organize things simply, to avoid chaos, emotional hunger, and impulsive decisions.

Routine, Shopping, Light Batch Cooking

- **Routine**: Choose 3 fixed moments in your day to dedicate to small rituals (e.g., morning drink, stabilizing lunch, evening herbal tea).
- **Shopping**: Make a weekly list organized by function, not just food type. Example: foods for de-bloating, light proteins, healthy fat sources, natural salts, fermented items.
- **Light Batch Cooking**: Just 2 hours a week is enough to prep:
    - 2 grain bases (e.g., rice and oats)
    - 2 proteins (e.g., hard-boiled eggs and hummus)
    - 2 cooked vegetables
    - 1 smart condiment
    - 1 broth or ready-to-eat soup

What to Prep in Advance
- Bottled Pink Salt Water for 3 days
- Vegetable broth with Pink Salt to sip or use in meals
- Toasted seed mix, hummus, freezer-friendly soups
- Smoothie "starter packs" with pre-portioned ingredients in the freezer

How to Adapt Meals Based on Energy and Mood

STATE	WHAT TO EAT
Bloated and sluggish	Detox waters + cooked vegetables + mineral broth with Pink Salt
Hungry but drained	Eggs, avocado, rich condiments + Pink Salt
Sugar cravings	Chia seed pudding, dark chocolate + pink salt
Mentally active	Cool, fresh dishes with citrus, herbs, and fermented foods
Emotionally intense day	Light comfort foods: polenta, squash, risottos with Pink Salt

The Science Behind It

The Pink Salt Method is grounded in body awareness, but it also has clear, documented scientific foundations. Here you'll find supporting insights that explain why it works—and why it can become a sustainable habit.

Studies on Hydration and Metabolism
- Intracellular hydration (not just "drinking a lot") is essential for hormonal, digestive, and mental regulation.
- Research shows that small amounts of natural salts (sodium + potassium + magnesium) help water absorption, reducing fatigue and water retention.
- Controlled use of Pink Salt promotes a shift from insulin spikes to stable blood sugar levels.

Insights on pH, Minerals, and Hormones

- The body's pH is supported by foods rich in alkaline minerals: fruits, vegetables, living water, broths with Pink Salt.
- Pink Salt does not "raise blood pressure" in an inflamed body: it remineralizes and regulates, especially when paired with water, magnesium, and gentle movement.
- Pink Salt contains trace amounts of iron, calcium, and potassium—helpful during hormonal stress, menstruation, or after fasting.

Updated Sources and Useful Resources

List of Studies:

- American Journal of Clinical Nutrition – "Sodium and potassium balance in active women"
- Frontiers in Endocrinology – "The metabolic reset: hydration, salt and hormonal balance"
- Harvard School of Public Health – "Salt, stress and adrenal recovery"

Weekly Body Awareness Journal

On this journey, calories don't matter—connections do.

I'm not asking you to weigh your food, but to weigh the impact it has on you.

This journal accompanies you for one week, one page per day, with prompts to answer honestly—not to be "good," but to understand yourself better.

You can print it, copy it into a notebook, or simply use it as daily inspiration. The goal is not to do it perfectly, but to do it authentically.

Day ___

How do I feel upon waking up?

(energy, bloating, mood, hunger, sleep...)

→ _____

What ritual did I choose today?

(a drink, a recipe, a walk, a quiet moment...)

→ _____

Did I respond to true hunger or mental hunger?

(be honest, no judgment)

→ _____

One thing I did for my body today:

(it can be something small: drinking water, taking a breath before eating, not finishing the plate just to finish it...)

→ _____

A phrase or thought that helped me stay centered:

(it can be your own or something you read)

→ _____

Weekly Reflection

At the end of the week, take ten minutes to read through your entries.

You may notice patterns, recurring signals, foods or rituals that supported you.

Don't look for right or wrong—look for what feels good.

Guiding Question:

What truly made me feel good?

→ _____

And what do I want to carry with me into next week?

→ _____

This is an example of how my weekly journal is structured.

You can choose to write this in your own notebook or journal, or copy it into a PDF and print it out for as long as you need it to support your journey.

FAQ (With Real, Practical Answers)

Straightforward answers to the most frequently asked questions:

- **"What if I have high blood pressure?"**

→ You don't need to eliminate Pink Salt—just manage it. Use it in small amounts and always pair it with water and potassium (e.g., cooked vegetables, avocado).

- **"What if I skip a day?"**

→ Nothing falls apart. The body remembers consistency, not perfection. Gently pick it back up at the next moment.

- **"What if I don't see results?"**

→ Listen to your body, not just the scale. Often, the first results are mental: less bloating, more presence, clearer hunger cues.

- **"Can I use other salts?"**

→ Yes, but Pink Salt is richer in minerals. Refined salts don't support the reactivation process.

- **"How much Pink Salt per day?"**

→ From a pinch up to 1 teaspoon spread out over the day—always with plenty of water.

CONCLUSION

If you've made it this far, thank you.

Thank you, because reading is not something to take for granted. Changing is even less so. And you chose to be here, to try, to put yourself out there.

Maybe you saw yourself in some of these pages. Maybe you realized that the problem isn't you, but a system that made you believe you always had to fix something. And maybe, for the first time, you've started truly listening to yourself—without judgment.

This isn't an easy path. But it's a real one. And most importantly: it's yours. No magic formulas, no perfection to achieve. Just presence, listening, and small acts repeated with intention.

Keep going. Even when you stumble. Even when it feels like you're back at square one. Because you're not. Every time you choose to begin again, you're moving forward. Consistency matters more than motivation. Kindness toward yourself matters more than rigidity.

A special thank-you goes to all the people who inspired these pages: those who shared their experiences, asked questions, tried and tried again. This book was born for you, but above all, with you.

Take it with you—not as a manual to follow to the letter, but as a tool to adapt to your own life. Make it yours. Personalize it. Change it. But don't abandon yourself.

Everything you need is already within you. Now it's just a matter of practicing it.

I'm rooting for you.

Made in United States
Orlando, FL
31 July 2025